THE VICTORIA HISTORY OF MIDDLESEX

ST CLEMENT DANES: 1660–1900

Edited by Francis Calvert Boorman

with Jonathan Comber and Mark Latham

VICTORIA COUNTY HISTORY

First published 2018

A Victoria County History publication

© The University of London, 2018

ISBN 978-1-909646-79-7

Cover image: Medieval houses in Wych Street, overlooked by the tower of St Clement Danes church in 1851 © The Trustees of the British Museum.
Back cover image: Royal Courts of Justice © University of London.

Typeset in Minion Pro by Lianne Sherlock and Jessica Davies Porter

CONTENTS

LIST OF ILLUSTRATIONS

Tables

Data for tables taken from the Westminster Historical Database.

ACKNOWLEDGEMENTS

THIS BOOK HAS BEEN SOMETHING of a relay race, with different sections written by different authors at different times. I only ran the last leg, in adding the final sections and drawing the material together, so I have to start by thanking Mark Latham and Jonathan Comber for handing on their excellent contributions for me to work with.

All of us benefitted hugely from the help and support of the teams at various libraries and archives, although two particularly stood out. Firstly, the Westminster Archives Centre holds many of the primary sources we all consulted and their staff were unfailingly helpful. Jonathan Comber worked on the records of the Holborn Estate Charity there and extends his thanks to Keith Rea, chief executive of the Westminster Amalgamated Charity, for giving him access. I also made extensive use of the rare books and music room at the British Library and I am grateful for their expertise and accommodation.

While the vast repository of parish archives available on the London Lives website wasn't available when a lot of our research took place, I am still very thankful for how much easier it made checking and revising material, along with numerous other internet sources. We historians are increasingly standing on the shoulders of gigantic digitised repositories and their creators.

I would like to thank Miles Taylor and Elizabeth Williamson, who got me involved in this project in the first place, and everyone at the Victoria County History, past and present, who has helped with comments, suggestions and at various stages of production, including Angus Winchester, Richard Hoyle, Patricia Croot, Lianne Sherlock, Adam Chapman, Jessica Davies Porter and Matthew Bristow. Peter Maplestone was very generous in sharing his own research on the parish. My dad Steve Boorman gets special mention for assisting with spreadsheets, without any (professional) interest or obligation to do so.

Finally, this volume could never have been produced without the financial support of the Westminster History Club. The Club's organisers who wrote the foreword to this book have already thanked all the many other contributors to the Club, but they also deserve recognition for their hard work, inventiveness, commitment and enthusiasm for local history.

FOREWORD

IT IS WITH GREAT PLEASURE that the organisers of the Westminster History Club have been asked to write the foreword for this prestigious publication on the parish of St Clement Danes.

For many the big red books of the *Victoria History of the County of Middlesex* are an invaluable resource and a guide to delving more deeply into their local history. This work on St Clement Danes is a new venture, part of the VCH Shorts series, bringing aspects of the history of Westminster's parishes to a wide audience and supplementing the histories of Westminster's landownership and religious life covered in *VCH Middlesex XIII* (2009).

This Westminster VCH Short is the first individual scholarly account of the history of St Clement Danes parish. It provides lively yet richly detailed accounts of the built environment, local government, charities, schools, and of economic and social life. Through it we can deepen our understanding of this ancient and diverse area, influenced by its position between the City of London and the national and commercial hearts of Westminster. The writers have scrupulously unpicked the development of its complicated institutions and charted the fluctuating fortunes of the parish, referring to an impressive range of sources and enlivening the story with local characters like John Dent, the unfortunate policer of morality, and Elizabeth Twining, locally known for her charitable works but more widely recognisable as a member of the family of tea merchants.

The City of Westminster Council was, for many years, a generous supporter of the VCH. After changes to funding in 2011, the Westminster History Club was formed to carry on raising funds and continues to support research and kindle enthusiasm for the history of the area through convivial talks. The Club was inaugurated by past Lord Mayor Councillor Judith Warner, with Councillor Gwyneth Hampson and Elizabeth Williamson, former Executive Editor of the VCH, and has been supported by successive Lord Mayors of the City. We would like to thank all those who have already attended, enjoying topics which ranged from the devastating Great Fire of 1834 that burned down Parliament, brilliantly recounted by Caroline Shenton, to the marvels of Westminster Abbey, lovingly described by David Carpenter. The enthusiasm and generosity of our speakers and of those who joined us for the talks have made this book possible.

It has been a pleasure for us, as organisers of the Club, to work alongside the Victoria County History team, in particular Francis Boorman, one of the main researchers and writers of this fascinating book. We are sure you will agree that this small but illuminating volume has made everybody's hard work worthwhile and with one Middlesex title published, *Knightsbridge and Hyde*, and further projects already planned, such as the history of St George Hanover Square, we hope you will continue to support Victoria County History.

Gwyneth Hampson, Catherine Longworth, Judith Warner and Elizabeth Williamson
On behalf of the Westminster History Club

INTRODUCTION

THE LATE 17TH-CENTURY CHURCH of St Clement Danes remains in the middle of the Strand as the central church of the Royal Air Force. Some houses from a similar period can also be found on Essex Street, but there are few other clues that this was a parish which had, until the late 19th century, been home to some of the best-preserved medieval buildings in London.[1] Reconstruction began in the second half of the 19th century, with the huge development of the Victoria Embankment and particularly the erection of the Royal Courts of Justice. In *Some Account of the Parish of St Clement Danes* of 1868, John Diprose noted how 'the character of the parish is being rapidly changed by the wholesale demolition of houses and streets', prompting him to chronicle the ancient fabric being swept away.[2] As the 19th century came to a close, the process was well-advanced and the layout of streets found in the early 21st century was established.

In 1900, the civil parish of St Clement Danes was superseded by the London County Council, which was responsible for completing the rebuilding of most of the area covered by the parish. In 2018, the part of London that had been St Clement Danes parish was dominated by large, thrusting buildings from the zenith of the Victorian and Edwardian empire, including the developments already mentioned, as well as Aldwych and Kingsway. An area that was once made up of a mix of residential and commercial buildings was replaced by universities and offices, although it still remains sandwiched between the districts of 'legal London' to the east and 'Theatreland' to the west.

This book charts the changing nature of the parish from the Restoration of 1660 up to 1900. Part One describes the built environment of the parish. In the Middle Ages until the 16th century, St Clement Danes was the site of grand, aristocratic riverside houses.[3] A first period of rebuilding in the 1670s and 1680s led to the area being characterised by its population of middling artisans and lawyers. Then came a steady decline until the parish had large areas of slum housing in the 19th century. This part also identifies the concomitant developments in the economic life of the parish, using occupational data to show how the typical resident changed along with the types of housing available and the influence of city-wide trends.

Part Two on local government explains how the vestry operated within the complexities of Westminster politics, providing policing, street cleaning and poor relief with varying degrees of success, under the demographic pressures of a rapidly growing metropolis. The poor were also looked after by the St Clement Danes Holborn Estate Charity whose

1   S. Bradley and N. Pevsner, *The Buildings of England, London 6: Westminster* (2003), 289–91, 346–7.
2   J. Diprose, *Some Account of the Parish of Saint Clement Danes (Westminster) Past and Present*, I (1868), iii.
3   P. Croot, 'A Place in Town in Medieval and Early Modern Westminster: The Origins and History of the Palaces in the Strand', *The London Journal*, 39:2 (2014), 85–101.

funding and activities are detailed. The parish provided schools, whose rich history is made all the more interesting as their successors were still operating in 2018.

The final part of the book places these architectural and institutional changes within a social context and shows how the activities and aspirations of the parishioners shifted over the centuries. This third section details the lively political and religious histories of the parish. We are introduced to Westminster politicians, from Charles James Fox to W.H. Smith, and may even hear the echo of the famed marrow-bone-and-cleaver music played by the Clare Market butchers.

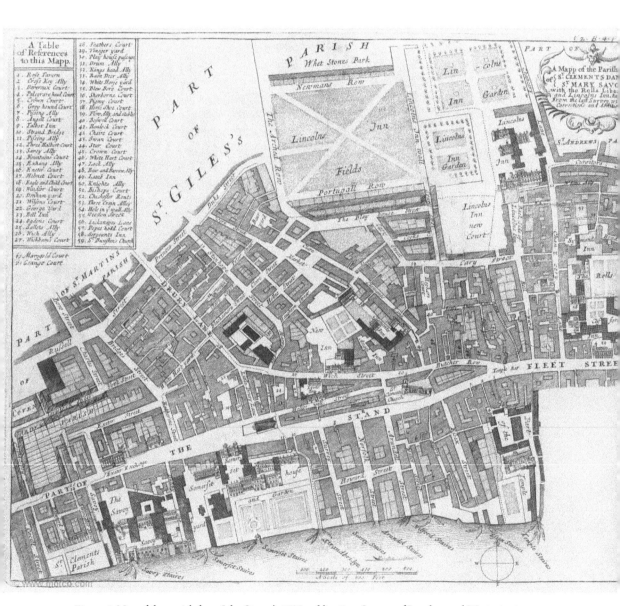

Figure 1 *Map of the parish from John Strype's 1720 publication,* Survey of London and Westminster.

Origins and Boundaries

THE AREA THAT BECAME THE parish of St Clement Danes lay to the west of Roman Londinium, but later lay within the area identified as the Anglo-Saxon settlement of Ludenwic, probably from the 7th century. Evidence of industrial activity, including iron and bronze furnace slag, has been found nearby at Covent Garden.[1] St Clement Danes was one of the four ancient Westminster parishes, first recorded in the 1190s.[2] The medieval parish lay partly in the vill of Westminster, a manor held by Westminster Abbey, and partly in the soke belonging to the earl of Leicester.[3] The soke subsequently became part of the Duchy of Lancaster's liberty, also known as the Savoy.

Thanks to these medieval antecedents, and the creation of the City of Westminster in 1585, the parish of St Clement Danes straddled two separate administrative entities.[4] Approximately half the parish of St Clement Danes lay within Westminster. The other half – a significant part of the main parish including the island in the Strand on which the parish church stands, plus most of the detached section of the parish to the west – lay within the Liberty of the Savoy which, by the 18th century, comprised an area bounded by the Thames on the south, Cecil Street to the west, the City of London to the east, and the Strand to the north (excepting one block north of the Strand to Essex Street, where the Lyceum Theatre lay in the 18th century).[5] The boundary of the eastern section of the parish ran north from the border with the City of London through the middle of Great Shire Lane, turning east in the middle of Lincoln's Inn New Square and then following Portugal Street to its north. The boundary turned south-west in the middle of Duke Street, excluding Princes Street to the north-west, followed the centre of Drury Lane and Wych Street south-east, passing just east of St Mary-le-Strand church and then south through the centre of Strand Lane.

The historic structure of the parish, split between Westminster and the Savoy, meant that by the 17th century, five principal bodies claimed jurisdiction over various aspects of local government in St Clement Danes. Two of these bodies: the parish vestry and the Middlesex and Westminster Justices of the Peace (JPs), claimed jurisdiction over

---

1   F. Sheppard, *London: A History* (Oxford, 1998), 58–62.
2   *VCH Middx* XIII, 162. A fifth ancient parish, Holy Innocents, did not survive as a separate entity after the 13th century. *VCH Middx* XIII, 8.
3   *VCH Middx* XIII, 7, 162.
4   *VCH Middx* XIII, 37–41. The duchy continued to be administered as a separate entity until 1899.
5   BL, Maps Crace Port. 13.54, *Map of the Manor of the Savoy and the Liberty of the Duchy of Lancaster called the Savoy Liberty in the county of Middlesex* (1830); R. Somerville, *Savoy* (1960), 152–3 and front endpaper, J. Rocque, *Map of the Savoy Manor and Liberty* (1740).

the entire parish. The jurisdiction of the three other bodies, the Westminster Court of Burgesses, the Court of Burgesses of the Duchy Liberty and the court leet or manorial court of the Duchy Liberty with its bailiff and steward, was restricted to those parts of the parish covered by their respective liberties. For administrative purposes, each of the two liberties contained four wards. The Duchy Liberty contained the Royal Ward, Middle Ward, Savoy Ward and Church Ward. The Westminster Liberty (by far the larger of the two liberties in terms of number of households) contained Holywell Ward, Drury Lane Ward, Sheer Lane Ward and Temple Bar Ward.[6]

These wards, similar to the precincts of the City of London, were probably sub-divisions of the sixteen original wards created for the administrative purposes of the Court of Burgesses (each burgess was responsible for a ward) in the late 16th century.[7] The eight wards became a cornerstone of parochial governance in St Clement Danes by the 18th century, and they formed the lowest level of administrative unit within the parish. Exactly when these wards were created is not clear: the first mention of them in the St Clement Danes vestry minutes occurs in 1702.[8]

Population

Estimates for the population of St Clement Danes before 1600 are hard to come by, but the parish was badly affected by the Great Plague of 1665, when hundreds of people in the area died.[9] Using data gathered from the 4*s*. in the pound tax of 1694, the population in St Clement Danes was put at 9,920, declining to 7,221 by 1739, according to William Maitland's *History of London*. A much higher estimate of population, using the bills of mortality, suggests 13,425 people in 1690, declining to 10,960 in the 1700s, then increasing to a high of 14,500 in 1730. Numbers then declined significantly to just under 8,000 in 1761.[10] These figures may be an underestimate, or the population may have picked up by 1801, when there were 12,861 people in the area.[11]

In the early 19th century, the number of people increased by almost 1,000 every ten years, reaching a peak of around 15,500 in 1831, and fluctuating by fewer than 100 people each decade until 1861. The next ten years were shaped by the slum clearances on the site of the new Royal Courts of Justice in the east of the parish. Between 1866 and 1868, the area including Boswell Court, Ship Yard and Serle's Place was cleared, displacing over 4,000 people. By 1871, the population of the parish was 11,503.[12] At the same time, the number of inhabited buildings fell from 1,456 to 1,102, meaning that the number of inhabitants per household fell slightly, from 10.63 in 1861 to 10.44 in 1871.[13] Population decline continued through the final three decades of the 19th century, although Charles Booth identified a 'considerable floating population' in the area who

6   E. Hatton, *A New View of London*, I (1708), 207.
7   B. Webb and S. Webb, *English Local Government: the Manor and the Borough* (1906), 218 n.2.
8   WCA, St CD Vestry Mins, B1061, 5 & 13 Aug. 1702.
9   W. Thornbury, *Old and New London*, III (1878), 10–15.
10   'St Clement Danes', https://www.londonlives.org/static/StClementDane.jsp#toc4 (accessed 6 June 2017).
11   *Census*, 1801.
12   'Table of population, 1801–1901', *VCH Middx* II, 119.
13   *Census*, 1871.

snatched sleep where they could and were not picked up by the census.[14] By 1901, St Clement Danes was home to only 6,010 people.[15]

Communications

Until the 19th century, routes through the parish were focused on the principal east–west thoroughfares, the Strand and the river. It was not until the second half of the 18th century that significant improvements were made to the street environment in much of the parish. These were undertaken by the newly instituted commission for cleaning, lighting and paving Westminster, set up by various Acts of Parliament during the 1760s.[16] The repaving of the Strand was particularly well-received. The *Annual Register* grandly announced 'that no Street in London, paved, lighted, and filled with signs fixed in the old way ever made so agreeable an appearance, or afforded better walking as the Strand does in the new'.[17] The authorities in the City of London were soon shamed into emulating the improvements in Westminster; driving a coach along the Strand in St Clement Danes, through Temple Bar and into the City was described as like 'going out into a boisterous sea, from a calm and peaceful river'.[18] Despite its success, the vestry governments covered by the commission did not appreciate its usurpation of their rate-gathering powers and it was dismantled in a piecemeal fashion, as various streets and parishes regained independent control of their paving and lighting.[19] Even after the construction of the Victoria Embankment (1864–70), vehicular traffic on the Strand remained 'continuous', but changed in composition as cabs lost their City monopoly in 1832 and were gradually replaced by cheaper horse buses as the more popular mode of transport.[20] The dominant bus provider in the late 19th century was the London General Omnibus Company, established in 1856.[21] Horse buses increased their capacity by adding roof seating in the 1840s.[22] Despite the emergence of motor cabs, horse-drawn 'Growlers' could still be sighted in the Strand in the 1920s.

Victoria Embankment

The Victoria Embankment was constructed between 1864 and 1870. Upon opening it provided a new roadway, as well as the completion of a much-needed sewerage system and underground railway. Designed and built by the Metropolitan Board of Works (MBW), it was an example of what could be achieved by a coherent planning body.[23]

---

14   LSE, Booth Collection, B340, 3.
15   'Table of population, 1801–1901', *VCH Middx* II, 119.
16   M. Ogborn, *Spaces of Modernity: London's Geographies, 1680–1780* (New York, 1998), 91–103; J. White, *London in the Eighteenth Century: A Great and Monstrous Thing* (2012) 61–3.
17   *The Annual Register, or a view of the history, politicks, and literature, for the year 1765* (1766), 110.
18   *Gazetteer and New Daily Advertiser*, 9 Oct. 1765.
19   P. Langford, *Public Life and the Propertied Englishman, 1689–1798* (Oxford, 1991), 454–5.
20   Diprose, *Some Account*, 95.
21   S. Taylor (ed.), *The Moving Metropolis: A History of London's Transport Since 1800* (2001), 51.
22   Ibid., 73.
23   J. White, *London in the Nineteenth Century: 'A human awful wonder of God'* (2007), 46–55.

Figure 2 *The Embankment in 1874, looking east from the terrace of Somerset House, as a regiment of Grenadiers marches into the parish.*

The Embankment transformed the riverside section of St Clement Danes parish, which became home to Temple station, of the Metropolitan District Railway and the new Temple Pier.[24] Opposite the new Temple Gardens, there was even a small patch of greenery complete with a bandstand, while the western riverside section was no longer a commercial space but part of Victoria Embankment Gardens.[25]

Kingsway

A similar transformation in the provision of a new north–south route, Kingsway, was not achieved until the beginning of the 20th century. The idea for a north–south thoroughfare connecting Holborn to the Strand had been suggested as long ago as 1766, in John Gwynn's *London and Westminster Improved*.[26] The plan to build a road starting at Southampton Row and ending near Somerset House was floated in 1836, and repeatedly resurfaced in various guises throughout the 19th century.[27] The vestry of St Clement Danes lobbied the MBW for a similar scheme in 1875, proposing the creation of a thoroughfare between the Strand and Holborn, via Lincoln's Inn and Clare Market.[28] The London County Council Improvements (Holborn to Strand) Act (1899) provided for a

24   Diprose, *Some Account*, 226–30.
25   See the OS map of London (1869–80) at https://www.locatinglondon.org overlaid on John Rocque's 1746 map of London, OS 5 ft to the mile, 1st edn.
26   J. Gwynn, *London and Westminster Improved* (1766), 99 and fold-out maps.
27   LCC, *Opening of Kingsway and Aldwych by His Majesty the King, Accompanied by Her Majesty the Queen* (1905), 4.
28   WCA, St CD Vestry Mins, B1082, 24 Feb. 1875, 2 June 1875, 3 July 1875.

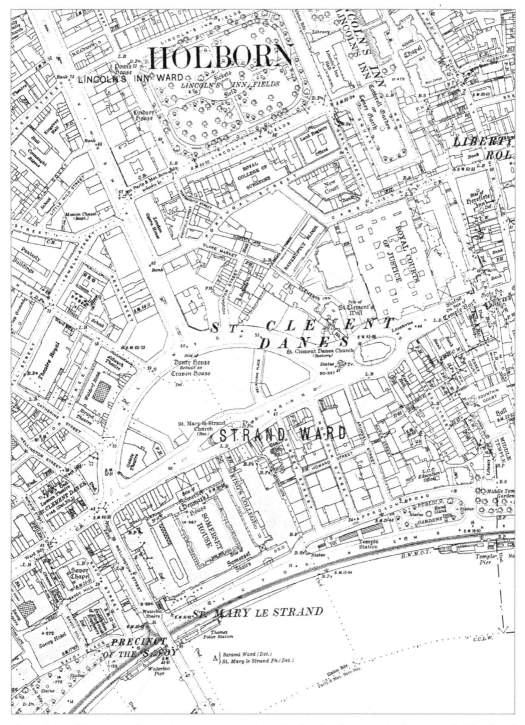

Figure 3 *Detail from an Ordnance Survey map revised in 1914 showing the recent developments of Aldwych and Kingsway.*

new road called Kingsway that would travel south from High Holborn and then bifurcate at Stanhope Street to create Aldwych, with the western branch providing an approach to Waterloo Bridge, while the eastern branch would join the Strand at St Clement Danes Church. Both Kingsway (1800 ft long) and Aldwych (1500 ft long) were 100 ft wide. The new Aldwych–Kingsway route was opened by the King and Queen on 18 October 1905. The *Illustrated London News* trumpeted that 'London has known no improvement of equal importance since Regent Street was built more than eighty years ago'.[29] Its construction allowed developments in public transport although trams did not reach the parish of St Clement Danes until the Kingsway Tram Subway was opened in 1906. The extension of tramways into central London was rejected by Parliament in 1872.[30] Due to difficulties in receiving the necessary permissions, the tunnel did not include an extension underneath the Embankment until 1908 and trams terminated at Aldwych. Tracks were also laid across Westminster Bridge in 1906 and the completed line formed the first link between the tramways in the north and south of the capital.[31]

Settlement and Built Environment

St Clement Danes was a large urban parish which was relatively wealthy, although it was characterised by a mixed population of rich and poor, and possessed various distinctive neighbourhoods. These included some very attractive areas with desirable housing, like several of the streets leading from the Strand down to the Thames. There were also some extremely narrow courts and alleys such as those surrounding Clare Market, in which the buildings gradually deteriorated between 1660 and the middle of the 19th century, by which time they were dilapidated, densely populated slums. There were two important periods of change to the built environment of St Clement Danes: firstly in the late 17th century, when new streets were laid out in place of the large houses near to the Thames and the parish church was rebuilt. Few building projects of note were undertaken in the 18th century, but several sites, particularly by the river, were converted for industrial and commercial usage. In the late 19th century, swathes of very old housing were knocked down and replaced by the Royal Courts of Justice, and the Victoria Embankment transformed the riverside sections of the parish once again, before the construction of Aldwych and Kingsway completed the slum clearances.

The 17th Century

The major landmarks in St Clement Danes included Clare Market, which ended the City monopoly in markets when it was built in 1657.[32] The market was named after the 2nd earl of Clare, John Holles (d. 1666), whose family was linked to the names of several

29   *Illustrated London News*, 21 Oct. 1905.
30   J.R. Day, *London's Trams and Trolleybuses* (1977), 6.
31   S. Taylor (ed.), *The Moving Metropolis: a History of London's Transport Since 1800* (2001), 132–3.
32   J. Howell, *Londonopolis: An historical discourse or perlustration of the City of London* (1657), 344–5; C.S. Smith, 'The market place and the market's place in London, *c*.1660–1840', (Univ. London, unpubl. PhD, 1999), 58.

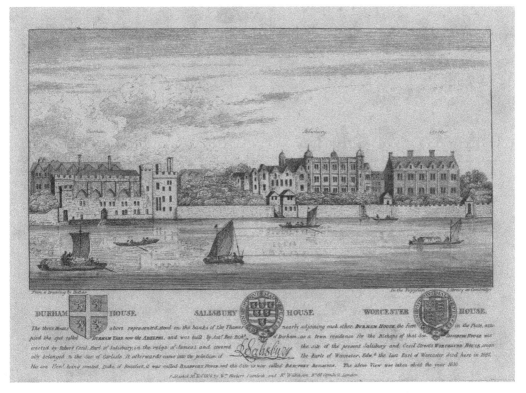

Figure 4 *View from the river Thames from around 1630, with Durham House on the left, Salisbury House in the centre and Worcester House on the right.*

streets in this area of the parish, including Holles Street, Houghton Street and Denzill Street.[33] The parish was also home to Clement's Inn, New Inn and Lyon's Inn, which were all Inns of Chancery dating from at least the 15th century.[34] Lincoln's Inn Fields, to the north-east, was already well-defined, but the surrounding area continued to fill with houses.[35] Further east near Temple Bar, and in the middle of the Strand, was the row of tenements fronting both to the north and south, called Butchers' Row.[36] Nearby was the parish church, also in the middle of the Strand. Essex and Arundel Houses, named for the respective earls, with their large, ornate gardens looking over the Thames, lay south of the Strand.[37] The episcopal palaces, Worcester and Salisbury Houses were also south of the Strand, but in the separate western section of the parish.[38] The parish was just west of the huge swathes of the City destroyed in the Great Fire of 1666; the flames reached the Temple, very close to its eastern border. It is likely that some of the buildings along the

33 W.M. Stern, 'Clements Inn Passage (Clare Market) 1687–1921', *The Genealogists' Mag.*, 15:13 (1968), 481.
34 H.S. Steel, 'Origin and history of English Inns of Chancery', *The Virginia Law Reg.*, 13:8 (1907), 585–93.
35 J. Summerson, *Georgian London* (1970), 20.
36 Howell, *Londinopolis*, 347.
37 *Ogilby and Morgan's Large Scale Map of the City As Rebuilt By 1676* ([s.l.], 1676), *British History Online*: https://www.british-history.ac.uk/no-series/london-map-ogilby-morgan/1676/map (accessed 1 May 2017).
38 Howell, *Londinopolis*, 348–9.

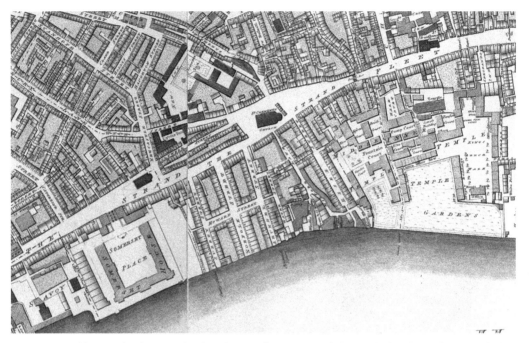

Figure 5 *Detail from Richard Horwood's Plan, showing the area around the parish church. Butcher's Row had been recently cleared and Newcastle Street constructed.*

Strand which were unroofed or even partially demolished to prevent the fire spreading any further west were in St Clement Danes.[39]

Although the damage done by the Great Fire in the parish was comparatively small, the parish experienced some of the effects from the wave of new building that occurred in London during the two decades after the fire. Firstly, a new gate was erected at Temple Bar in 1670 and its embellishment completed by 1672.[40] Major reconstruction occurred south of the Strand, where the string of large houses were passed on to a new generation or sold, and then demolished and replaced by streets. Their owners moved north and west to fashionable new developments, bringing the 'aristocratic age' of the Strand to a close.[41] Essex House, damningly described by Pepys as 'large, but ugly', was sold following the death of its owner, Frances Devereux, dowager duchess of Somerset in 1674, and apparently valued at £7,000.[42] Charles II agreed to buy it for £12,000 for the earl of Essex, but somehow word of the purchase got out and a major London developer, Dr Nicholas Barbon, secured a contract before Essex could.[43] Essex pleaded with the King not to grant a building licence for the site and Barbon was even summoned before the Privy Council and pressured by the King, but Barbon had already started digging up the garden before

39   J. Evelyn, *Diary and Correspondence of John Evelyn, F.R.S*, II (1850), 12.

40   Hatton, *London*, I, ix.

41   L. Stone 'The residential development of the West End of London in the seventeenth century', in B.C. Malament (ed.), *After the Reformation: Essays in honour of J.H. Hexter* (Manchester, 1980), 195.

42   *Samuel Pepys' Diary*, 24 Jan. 1669; C.L. Kingsford, 'Essex House, formerly Leicester House and Exeter Inn', *Archaeologia*, LXXIII (1923), 15; *Essex Papers* (1838) 226.

43   *Essex Papers*, 299, 309–11.

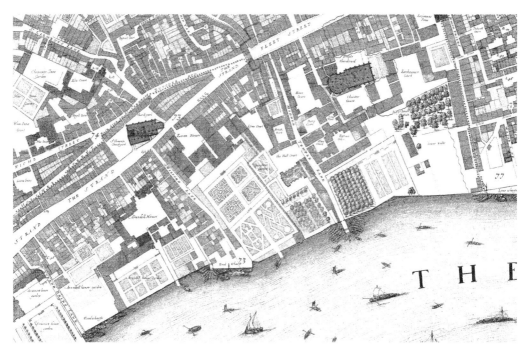

Figure 6 *Detail from Ogilby and Morgan's map of 1676, showing Arundel and Essex houses south of the Strand, with their large gardens stretching down to the Thames.*

the site was formally conveyed and continued building without heed.[44] He tore down Essex House and replaced it with Devereux Court and Essex Street, while the gardens were turned into wharves for woodmongers and brewers.[45]

In 1671 Henry, Lord Howard obtained an Act of Parliament for building and improving the grounds of Arundel House and the King granted a piece of soil 40 ft in depth between Strand Bridge and Milford Stairs to extend the garden.[46] Between 1678 and 1682, Arundel House was pulled down by Lord Howard, and the partially constructed Arundel, Surrey, and Norfolk Streets can be seen on a map of 1682, when Howard still intended to rebuild Arundel House on a reduced site which had been cleared.[47] Sir Christopher Wren designed a new house but it was never built, and another Act of Parliament was granted in around 1690, allowing leases to be issued for the garden ground. Arundel, Surrey and Norfolk Streets were then completed down to the Thames, with Howard Street bisecting them.[48] In the western section of the parish, Worcester House became Beaufort Buildings and Fountain Court in 1682–3, after the newly created duke of Beaufort moved to the duke of Buckingham's old house in Chelsea.[49] Little and Great Salisbury Houses were succeeded by Salisbury and Cecil Streets respectively

44 *Essex Papers*, 311–13, 322–4.
45 E.H. Reynolds (ed.), *Wells Cathedral: Its foundation, constitutional history and statutes* (1881), lxvii.
46 *Cal. SP Dom.*, 1676–7, 226.
47 W. Morgan, *London &c. Actually Surveyed* (1682).
48 C. Howard, *Historical Anecdotes of Some of the Howard Family* (1769), 110; C. Lethbridge Kingsford, 'Bath Inn or Arundel House', *Archaeologia*, LXII (1922), 243–77.
49 *VCH Middx* XIII, 50.

between the 1670s and 1690s.[50] Exeter Exchange was built to the north of the Strand in the late 17th century, although the New Exchange proved a more desirable shopping destination.[51] It was removed into the parish of St Mary-le-Strand with a total of around 45 houses on the east side of Burleigh Street by the Commissioners for Building Fifty New Churches in 1723, over the objections of the parishioners of St Clement Danes.[52] The tower of St Clement Danes Church was rebuilt in 1668–70, and was the only part retained when the church was demolished in 1680. It was rebuilt under the direction of Wren and completed in 1682.[53]

Dwellings were fairly large in the parish; in 1666, the mean average of hearths per dwelling was six, one of the highest in metropolitan London.[54] The parish was home to a relatively high number of gentry households partly drawn by the proximity of the Inns of Court, although their presence was more scattered than the clusters living further north and west. Women householders were less prevalent than in other parts of London, probably because of the commercial character of the area.[55] By 1693–4 there was little open space remaining and it was very densely populated, with 95.9 households/ha., compared with the Westminster mean of 13.7 and the City mean of 80.1.[56]

St Clement Danes lay in an area with the highest prosecution rates in metropolitan Middlesex. Rates of prosecution in the West End were high due to the social tension in these parishes, the willingness of richer residents to bear the cost of prosecution and the geographical proximity of a courthouse. The West End also had a high incidence of commitment to houses of correction, due to a larger proportion of prosecutions for vice offences, spurred on by the efforts of Societies for the Reformation of Manners. Prosecutions in St Clement Danes were still much lower than for its northern neighbour of St Giles in the Fields (8.1 per 1000 inhabitants compared to 13.0), probably due to St Clement Danes' greater social stability, which it maintained across the late 17th and early 18th century.[57] The Strand was a notable site of violence in the late 17th century and the Old Bailey recorded 13 trials of killings which took place there between 1675 and 1700. Five of these trials had a definite connection to St Clement Danes, three of the killings having taken place within the parish and two having been carried out by parishioners.[58] For example, Francis Rossington was found guilty of manslaughter and sentenced to branding in 1693, after a fight with Robert Fownes near the maypole in the Strand left Fownes with a 14 inch wound in his left buttock that proved fatal.[59]

---

50   Ibid., 51.

51   J. Strype, *A Survey of the Cities of London and Westminster*, II, iv, 7 (1720), 116.

52   M.H. Port (ed.), *The Commissions for Building Fifty New Churches: The Minute Books, 1711–27, A Calendar* (1986), 335, 12 July 1723; 339, 23 Sept. 1723.

53   Ibid., 166.

54   M.J. Power, 'The social topography of Restoration London', in A.L. Beier and R. Finlay (eds), *London 1500–1700*, 202–3; M. Davies et al (eds), *London and Middlesex 1666 Hearth Tax* (2014), 88.

55   C. Spence, *London in the 1690s: A social atlas*, (2000), 77–87.

56   Ibid., 176–8.

57   R. Shoemaker, *Prosecution and Punishment: Petty crime and the Law in London and Rural Middlesex, c.1660–1725* (Cambridge, 1991), ch. 10.

58   E.g. https://www.oldbaileyonline.org (accessed 17 Apr. 2011), 27 Feb. 1684, trial of Robert How (t16840227-8); 14 Oct. 1695, trial of John Stanford (t16951014-32).

59   https://www.oldbaileyonline.org (accessed 17 Apr. 2011), 6 Dec. 1693, trial of Francis Rossington (t16931206-34).

The 18th Century

In 1720 the parish was described as 'large, well built and inhabited, by many Persons both of the Nobility and Gentry, as well as rich Tradesmen'.[60] The completed Essex, Norfolk and Arundel Streets were not only described as 'regular and spacious' or 'pleasant and considerable'; they proved to be a sensible investment.[61] The new blocks of housing were far more profitable for their owners than the individual aristocratic dwellings that previously occupied their sites, increasing their rental income significantly; the ground rents were worth £480 a year in 1731.[62] Horse Shoe Court, Clare Court and Stanhope Street were all considered to be broad, open and spacious, while Vere Street attracted tradesmen of a respectable sort.[63] Clare Market, where a clerk rented the stalls from the duke of Newcastle, was well-stocked and desirable, selling both meat and fish; in 1773 it was still 'one of the best markets in town for all kinds of provisions'.[64] The fairly new buildings in the western section of the parish maintained their reputation for high quality and were mostly inhabited by the gentry in the end near the Thames, and tradesmen towards the Strand.[65] The parish church was improved in 1720, when its tower was raised by 25 ft and a new steeple 50 ft in height was installed.[66] The part of the Strand which passed through the parish was slightly narrower, with smaller houses, than it was further west, although it remained a very fashionable street for shopping along its entire length.[67]

At the same time, evidence from the Old Bailey trials suggests that the major thoroughfares in St Clement Danes continued to have very high rates of violent theft in the first half of the 18th century.[68] During the 1740s the number of recorded indictments had reached 1 per 139 inhabitants, comparing unfavourably with the London average of one indictment for every 305 people.[69] The reputation of the parish suffered from high profile crimes such as the murder of Peter Anthony Motteux, a French Huguenot dramatist and translator, in a bawdy house in Star Court, Butchers' Row in 1718.[70] Worse still, the six defendants were all from the parish and were characterised in the trial as the mistress of the house, three 'plyers' (prostitutes) of the house and the two men 'bullies to it' (pimps), though all were acquitted.[71]

---

60 Strype, *London and Westminster*, II, iv, 7, p. 116.
61 Hatton, *London*, I, 3, 59.
62 Strype, *London and Westminster*, II, iv, 7, p. 116; Howard, *Historical Anecdotes*, 110.
63 Strype, *London and Westminster*, II, iv, 7, pp. 118–9.
64 Ibid., 119; J. Noorthouck, 'Book 4, Ch. 3: The parishes of the Liberty of Westminster', *A New History of London: Including Westminster and Southwark* (London, 1773), 717–38: https://www.british-history. ac.uk/no-series/new-history-london/pp717-738 (accessed 29 Jan. 2014); C.S. Smith, 'The market place and the market's place in London, *c*.1660–1840', (Univ. London, unpubl. PhD, 1999), 122, 159.
65 Strype, *London and Westminster*, II, iv, 7, pp. 119–20.
66 *VCH Middx* XIII, 166.
67 H. Phillips, *Mid-Georgian London* (1964), 180.
68 'St Clement Danes', *LL*, https://www.londonlives.org/static/StClementDane.jsp#toc9 (accessed 21 Aug. 2014).
69 P. Linebaugh, 'Tyburn: A study of crime and the labouring poor in London during the first half of the 18th century', (Univ. Warwick, unpub. PhD, 1975), 2 vols, 60.
70 Old Bailey Proceedings, *London Lives, 1690–1800*: 23 Apr. 1718, trial of Edward Williams et al (t17180423-1); *London Gaz.*, 22–5 Mar. 1718.
71 D. Defoe, *The Political State of Great Britain*, XV (London, 1718), 425–36.

Figure 7 *Butcher's Row culminating in Temple Bar, which was removed then re-erected in Paternoster Square in 2004.*

The parish had a growing problem with prostitution. Both Drury Lane and the Strand, the latter a particularly busy area for streetwalkers, showed high concentrations of prostitution throughout the 18th century.[72] By the latter part of the 18th century, Westminster had also become the predominant district for bawdy houses in London.[73] In 1770–9 the number of disorderly houses in the Covent Garden area has been estimated at 241, which represented 71 per cent of the London total. St Clement Danes contained 32 of those 241.[74] A report of a committee of the House of Commons in 1770 took evidence

---

72　F.N. Dabhoiwala, 'Prostitution and police in London, c.1660–c.1760', unpublished PhD thesis (Oxford, 1995), 39; T. Henderson, *Disorderly Women in Eighteenth-Century London: Prostitution and control in the metropolis, 1730–1830* (1999), 59.

73　R. Trumbach, *Sex and the Gender Revolution: Heterosexuality and the third gender in enlightenment London*, I (1998), 120.

74　Trumbach, *Sex and the Gender Revolution*, I, 121–2.

from James Sayer, the Deputy High Steward of Westminster, stating that the majority of the most notorious unlicensed brothels and taverns in the capital were in the vicinity of Covent Garden; 30 were in St Mary-le-Strand, 12 in St Martin's and 12 in St Clement's.[75]

Local people did attempt to enforce the law and maintain higher moral standards in the area. John Dent lived in St Clement's and was the most famous of the Society for the Reformation of Manners' informers. He was known for 'aiding and assisting at the apprehending and prosecuting of several Thousands of Lewd and Profligate Persons' in a career spanning more than 17 years.[76] Dent died after attempting to intervene in the apprehension of a woman near Covent Garden who was presumed to be a prostitute, and being stabbed by three soldiers who took umbrage at the arrest.[77] Dent's funeral was held in St Clement Danes Church where a sermon was preached by Thomas Bray, founder of the Society for the Propagation of Christian Knowledge, and he was accompanied to his grave with 12 JPs as pall-bearers, 30 constables and beadles, over 20 clergymen and more than 1,000 mourners.[78] The court leet of the Duchy Liberty amerced numerous bawdy house keepers, demanding particularly large sums of up to £50 in the mid 18th century.[79]

Many streets had a mixed quality of housing stock, but the courts, passages and alleys in the parish were often very poor. By the mid 18th century, commerce had started to take over the riverfront and the area next to the Thames was occupied first by a timber yard and then two wharves by the 1790s.[80] Streets such as Milford Lane, leading from the Strand to the Thames, were overrun with commercial traffic bringing goods from the riverside wharves and were therefore less desirable and inhabited by poorer sorts. Other pockets of poor housing could be found in the courts north of the Strand, between St Clement Danes Church and Temple Bar, and the very old houses of Butchers' Row and Wych Street.[81] Butchers' Row was also home to a cluster of gin retailers, with at least 17 plying their trade in 1736.[82] Some of the less well-thought-of areas like Burleigh Street sounded respectable enough, but others were more descriptively named. The parish contained two Pissing Alleys. Strype felt that one of the alleys was named 'perhaps in contempt', while for the other, Pissing Alley was 'a very proper Name for it'.[83] Francis Place, a breeches maker and famed radical, grew up in the parish in the 18th century and colourfully described the poverty and low morals of various local tradesmen, most

75   J.P. Malcolm, *Anecdotes of the Manners and Customs of London*, I (2nd edn, 1810), 204.

76   Strype, *London and Westminster*, II, v, 3, p. 32.

77   *LL*, Middx Sess.: Sess. papers – justices' working docs, 19 Mar. 1709, LMSMPS501050014 (accessed 17 June 2012); T. Bray, *The tryals of Jeremy Tooley, William Arch, and John Clauson, three private soldiers. For the murder of Mr. John Dent, constable ... To which is added, a sermon preach'd at the funeral of Mr. John Dent* (1732).

78   Strype, *London and Westminster*, II, v, 3, p. 32; T. Bray, *The good fight of faith, in the cause of God against the kingdom of Satan. Exemplified in a sermon preach'd at the parish-church of St. Clements Danes, Westminster, on the 24th of March, 1708/9. At the funeral of Mr. John Dent, who was barbarously murder'd in the doing his duty, in the execution of the laws against profaneness and immorality* (1709).

79   Ritson, *A Digest of the Proceedings of the Court Leet of the Manor and Liberty of the Savoy* (1789), 13.

80   See John Rocque's 1746 map of London at https://www.locatinglondon.org and Horwood's 1792–9 map of London at https://www.motco.com (accessed 6 June 2017).

81   Strype, *London and Westminster*, II, iv, 7, pp. 117–8.

82   J. Warner, *Craze, Gin and Debauchery in an Age of Reason* (2003), 45.

83   Strype, *London and Westminster*, II, iv, 7, pp. 117–9.

of whom ended up leaving their family in distress.[84] St Clement Danes certainly had a varied population; many of its residents were migrants from all over England and Wales.[85]

In the second half of the 18th century, rebuilding occurred in Salisbury Street in 1765–73.[86] As so often happened in London, change to the street layout was brought about by disaster. In 1781 a fire broke out just east of the church of St Mary-le-Strand in the south-west corner of the parish of St Clement Danes, leaving an area of ruins behind a hoarding which was for a time occupied by 'a gang of young rascals and thieves', but was eventually rebuilt as Newcastle Street, running from the Strand to Clare Market.[87] Finally, some of the oldest, crumbling buildings in the parish were replaced. Butchers' Row was described in 1790 as 'a dirty place, composed of wretched fabrics and narrow passages, undeserving of the name of streets. The houses overhung their foundations, the receptacles of dirt and disease, and the bane of London'.[88] A reminder that poorly-maintained, ageing buildings could be dangerous, as well as ugly, came in 1796 when two houses collapsed, killing 16 people, in Houghton Street, Clare Market, which was sliding into decrepitude.[89] At around the same time, alderman and Lord Mayor William Pickett was campaigning for the removal of 'the decayed houses' at Butchers' Row.[90] They were purchased by the City of London and demolished, with the scheme sanctioned and refinanced by several Acts of Parliament from 1795 onwards.[91] The buildings put up in their place were dubbed Pickett Street and, largely finished by 1809, were sold by public lottery.[92] Previously the Strand, 'was in one part little better than a lane', but was made wider by the new development.[93]

The 19th Century

An insolvent debtors' court was planned for Portugal Street in a bill of 1822 and enlarged in the mid 19th century using unclaimed money, but it closed following the Bankruptcy Act of 1861 and was later used to hear compensation cases relating to the construction of the Royal Courts of Justice.[94] There were few further changes of note to the parish in the first half of the 19th century, other than the opening of King's College Hospital in 1840

---

84   M. Thale (ed.), *The Autobiography of Francis Place* (Cambridge, 1972), 87–9.

85   J. White, *London in the Eighteenth Century: A Great and Monstrous Thing* (2012), 90–1.

86   *VCH Middx* XIII, 51.

87   Thale (ed.), *The Autobiography of Francis Place*, 48; Diprose, *Some Account*, 180. For land ownership in this area see *VCH Middx* XIII, 87–8.

88   J.T. Smith, *An Antiquarian Ramble in the Streets of London: With anecdotes of their more celebrated residents*, I (1846), 375.

89   M.D. George, *London Life in the Eighteenth Century* (1965), 74.

90   W. Pickett, *Public Improvement; Or, a plan for making a convenient and handsome communication between the cities of London and Westminster* (1789), 3.

91   Listed in the Temple Bar Improvement Act, 49 Geo. III, c.82.

92   *The Strand Preparatory to its Improvement in the Year 1810* (1811), BM; 46 Geo. 3 c.97.

93   Thale (ed.), *The Autobiography of Francis Place*, 107.

94   *A bill to amend an act of the first year of His Present Majesty, for the relief of insolvent debtors in England Insolvent debtors court* (Parl. Papers 1822 (265) II), p.1053; *A bill to authorize the application of part of the unclaimed money in the Court for the Relief of Insolvent Debtors, in enlarging the court-house of the said court* (Parl. Papers 1847–8 (547) III), p. 286; Diprose, *Some Account*, 206.

and the addition of new buildings commenced in 1852, which were 'very much to the advantage of both the College and the neighbourhood'.[95] The main hospital building was also rebuilt and an improved passage made to the Strand, completed in 1861.[96] Despite evidence of improvement during the 1820s and early 1840s in the area around Clement's Inn Passage, much of the parish seemed to be in a general state of deterioration, to the extent that it was riddled with typhus, with the Clare Market neighbourhood worst affected.[97] Measles was rife in the 1850s.[98] Crowding in the area was hastened by developments to the west, such as Regent Street and Trafalgar Square, which pushed poor people into the Strand area. The number of inhabitants per household in the Strand district rose from 10.7 in 1831 to 11.4 in 1861, the second highest in London, which suggests a fall in the housing stock available in light of the stagnant population. The highest was in St Giles to the west (11.5) and the third highest in Holborn to the north (10.9).[99] Pockets of poor housing were rare in Westminster by this time and were confined to areas away from the main thoroughfares and with fragmented land ownership, such as the St Giles rookery and parts of St Clement Danes.[100] In 1850 the area around Clare Market continued to be a bustling mix of street stalls and provision shops, while in the market proper, 15 butchers sold high quality meat by day and then inferior meat to the poor in the evening.[101]

By the late 19th century, the slaughter of animals had all but died out in Clare Market and the produce was of much poorer quality, consisting of tallow, dried fish, unappetising vegetables and cheaper cuts of meat, which suited the purchasing power of local people.[102] A Parliamentary Select Committee tasked with looking into the paucity of resources for religious instruction in urban areas reported that the parish 'may in many respects be considered as the connecting medium between the two extremes of the highest and lowest of the London population'.[103] In 1858 the rector pointed out that of his estimate of 17,000 people in the parish, 10,000 were not rich enough to be ratepayers and that there were 'numbers of people swarming in one house – it is frightful'.[104] He also noted, 'the immense amount of spiritual destitution around', which was not confined to

95   E.J.C. Hearnshaw, *The Centenary History of King's College London 1828–1928* (1929), 229–30; Thornbury, *ONL*, III, 26–32.

96   Hearnshaw, *King's College London 1828–1928*, 230.

97   W.M. Stern, 'Clements Inn Passage (Clare Market) 1687–1921', *The Genealogists' Mag.*, 15:13 (1968), 487; M.D. George, *London Life in the Eighteenth Century* (1965), 85.

98   *Era*, 6 Jan. 1856.

99   D.R. Green, *From Artisans to Paupers: Economic change and poverty in London, 1790–1870* (Aldershot, 1995), 183, 185.

100 Ibid., 142.

101 H. Mayhew, *The Morning Chronicle Survey of Labour and the Poor: The metropolitan districts* (Horsham, 1982), 220.

102 C.S. Smith, 'The market place and the market's place in London, *c.*1660–1840', (Univ. London, unpubl. PhD, 1999), 58, 35; Thornbury, *ONL*, III, 36–44.

103 *Report from the Select Committee of the House of Lords, appointed to inquire into the deficiency of means of spiritual instruction and places of divine worship in the metropolis, and in other populous districts in England and Wales, especially in the mining and manufacturing districts; and to consider the fittest means of meeting the difficulties of the case; and to report thereon to the House; together with the proceedings of the committee, minutes of evidence, and appendix* (Parl. Papers, 1857–58 (387) ix), iv.

104 Ibid., 113, 116.

Figure 8 *Holywell Street in 1877. A gentleman browses a book display in the foreground.*

the 'worst streets in London' within his parish, but 'extends actually among the better classes'.[105]

By the 1860s, Clement's Lane was:

> … a narrow, stale-looking, crooked thoroughfare, filthy and inconvenient, the atmosphere redolent with the exhalations arising from a densely packed population, the majority of whom were of the grimy, grovelling class, living from hand to mouth by uncertain daily labour … Notwithstanding their decayed

105 Ibid., v.

and dilapidated appearance, however, many of these homes bore a palatial and noble aspect.[106]

The Strand was increasingly congested and the section between St Clement Danes and St Mary-le-Strand was a particular bottleneck.[107] The reputation of the parish seemed to be going the same way as its built environment. Holywell Street, described by one historian as 'a synecdoche for pornography' was known for the number of 'immoral' print and booksellers trading there, while the pornographers spilling over into Wych Street were jostling for trade with brothels, and the prostitutes touting for business in their doorways.[108]

In Vere Street, two men named Cook and Yardley rented the White Swan, 'a low, dirty public house, in the filthy avenues of Clare Market', and set it up as a molly house (where gay men could meet, socialise and have sex) in 1810.[109] Three rooms were decked out as a bedroom with four beds, a ladies' dressing room and a chapel, where mock weddings took place, frequently consummated by multiple couples.[110] Less than six months after it was opened, the White Swan was raided by three patrols of Bow Street officers. In all, 27 regular customers were taken to the St Clement Danes watch house, then removed to Bow Street to be examined, accompanied by an angry mob. Cook was convicted of keeping a disorderly house and six others were found guilty of attempted sodomy. They were sentenced to between one and two years in prison and to stand in the pillory in the Haymarket. The procession to the pillory went from Newgate prison and passed through St Clement Danes via the Strand. The prisoners suffered 'universal expressions of execration' and had all manner of filth thrown at them, from rotting vegetables to fish entrails and 'the remains of divers[e] dogs and cats'.[111] The repercussions of this notorious house at Vere Street and the subsequent trials were severe, and 'had a traumatising effect upon the gay subculture' of London.[112]

By the second half of the 19th century, new initiatives were underway to improve the moral and physical fabric of the parish.[113] Lord Campbell repeatedly invoked the 'filthy publications for sale in Holywell Street' whilst arguing for the Obscene Publications Act of 1857 in the House of Lords and, along with those in Wych Street, the proprietors of Holywell Street were the immediate target of arrests, seizures of prints and convictions after the act was passed.[114] Campbell compared his 'siege of Holywell Street' to the siege of Delhi.[115] The MBW was set up by Act of Parliament in 1855, finally providing a degree of supervision to improvement works in London that had been lacking since the slow

---

106 Diprose, *Some Account*, 169.

107 D.J. Olsen, 'Introduction: Victorian London', in D. Owen, *The Government of Victorian London 1855–1899* (Cambridge, Mass., 1982), 7.

108 I. McCalman, 'Unrespectable Radicalism: Infidels and pornography in early nineteenth-century London', *Past & Present*, 104 (1984), 107; Thornbury, *ONL*, III, 15–25, J. White, *London in the Nineteenth Century* (2008), 318.

109 R. Holloway, *The Phoenix of Sodom, or the Vere Street Coterie* (1813), 22.

110 Ibid., 10.

111 *The Morning Post*, 28 Sept. 1810.

112 R. Norton, *Mother Clap's Molly House* (1992), 186–98.

113 L. Nead, *Victorian Babylon: People, streets and images in nineteenth-century London* (2000), 165, 194–5.

114 146 *Parl. Debates*, 3rd Ser. 1153; *Daily News*, 23 Sept. 1857.

115 148 *Parl. Debates*, 3rd Ser. 227.

dwindling of the Westminster Paving Commission in the 18th century. St Clement Danes became part of the Strand district of the Board. It took nearly a decade for the MBW to undertake a major project, mainly due to vacillation in Parliament, but when work was finally undertaken, in the form of the Victoria Embankment, it was spectacular.[116]

Elsewhere in the parish, the decayed Lyon's Inn, where a murder occurred in 1823, was sold in 1868 and demolished to make way for two new theatres, the Globe that opened on to Newcastle Street and the Opera Comique, which had its frontage on the Strand.[117] The Norfolk estate, south of the Strand, was completely rebuilt during the 1880s for the first time since it was developed 200 years before.[118] The duke granted 80 year leases and advanced money to builders to facilitate the erection of offices and to widen Essex and Surrey Streets.[119] In the western part of the parish Beaufort Buildings were demolished and the Savoy Hotel built in their place.[120]

The new Royal Courts of Justice (originally the Law Courts), was also largely in the parish. Following lengthy controversy regarding the competition for the design and the choice of site, the building was finally opened in 1882, the year following the death of the architect, George Edmund Street.[121] Sandwiched between the Strand, Carey Street, Temple Bar and Clement's Inn, the area that was built over was notorious for its poor buildings and narrow alleys, some from before the Great Fire, and its undesirable inhabitants. There were some more respectable streets on the periphery of the site, however, and at least a quarter of inhabitants were not in fact so poor as to be deemed 'labouring class'.[122] The almshouses of the Holborn Estate Charity were also demolished. Nevertheless, at least part of the appeal of building here was the opportunity for 'the destruction of so many filthy slums'.[123] The site was also favoured by professional organisations such as the Law Society.[124] A site to the north of the new courts was also redeveloped. The Serle Street and Cook's Court Improvement Company was incorporated by Act of Parliament to rebuild the block of land bounded by Serle Street, Portugal Street and Carey Street as Court Chambers, to provide further accommodation for the legal profession.[125]

Writing in 1878, Thornbury thought Clare Market 'much improved' by philanthropic activity, including the addition of a new mission, schools and a working men's club along with other charitable institutions.[126] The local minister said in 1899 that there was little

---

116 F. Sheppard, *London 1808–1870: The Infernal Wen* (1971), 279–83.

117 Diprose, *Some Account*, 112; Thornbury, *ONL*, III, 15–25.

118 D.J. Olsen, *Town Planning in London, the Eighteenth and Nineteenth Centuries* (2nd edn, 1982), 190.

119 *Report from the Select Committee on Town Holdings* (Parl. Papers 1887 (260), xiii), 623–4.

120 *VCH Middx* XIII, 50.

121 D.B. Brownlee, *The Law Courts: The Architecture of George Edmund Street* (1984).

122 *Minutes of evidence taken before the Select Committee on the Courts of Justice Concentration (Site) Bill; with the proceedings of the committee* (Parl. Papers 1865 (124), xii), 383–401.

123 Thornbury, *ONL*, III, 15–25.

124 M. Port, 'From Carey Street to the Embankment – and back again!', *Lon. Top. Rec.* (1980), 167–90; M. Port, *Imperial London* (1995), ch. 7.

125 *Report of the commissioners appointed to advise and report as to the buildings proper to be erected, and the plans upon which such buildings shall be erected, for the new courts of justice* (Parl. Papers 1871 [C 290] xx), p.xxi; J. Diprose, *Some Account of the Parish of Saint Clement Danes (Westminster) Past and Present*, II (1876), 249.

126 Thornbury, *ONL*, III, 36–44.

Figure 9 *The imposing entrance to the Royal Courts of Justice, fronting onto the Strand.*

'actual prostitution' in the parish, but there were 'a good many loose women'.[127] Despite such immorality and a tendency toward heavy drinking in the poor of the parish, the minister found that, 'even in their wickednesses there was a certain "gentility"'.[128]

Into the 20th Century: Aldwych and Kingsway

It was not until the 1900s that the area was transformed completely, when Kingsway was built in the east of the parish. This finally created a large north–south thoroughfare through London, the antecedents of which stretched back to at least the mid 18th century. In 1866, at the beginning of the land clearances for the Royal Courts of Justice, the Medical Officer of Health (MOH) for the Strand, Dr Julian Hunter, summarised the difficulty of tackling poor living conditions in the area:

127 LSE, Booth Collection, B244, 199.
128 Ibid., 201.

Figure 10 *Detail from an Ordnance Survey map of 1878, showing the ground cleared for the Royal Courts of Justice, and the newly constructed Victoria Embankment and Temple Station.*

Experience shows that great metropolitan improvements, whereby houses in poorer neighbourhoods are demolished, by no means disperse the resident population in the manner which might be anticipated; but they tend rather to prove that in no considerable proportion, the families so displaced, merely migrate to the nearest courts and streets, and then provide themselves with homes, by converting the house, up to this time occupied by a single family, into one tenanted by nearly as many families as the rooms which it contains.[129]

Hunter's assessment continued to hold true for the rest of the 19th century. The cycle of overcrowding and slum clearances in St Clement Danes was only broken by the complete transformation of the area and loss of most of its residential character, when Aldwych and Kingsway were built from 1899.

With no provision made for their rehousing, many of the inhabitants of the slums that were cleared to make way for the Royal Courts of Justice had only moved as far as the Clare Market area, where the lanes and alleys 'are almost equally close and filthy, and sadly overcrowded'.[130] The destruction of high density slum housing without providing adequate alternatives led to the reshuffling, rather than eradication, of endemic overcrowding around the district. Charles Booth predicted its continuation in 1891: 'it is to be feared that the clearances made and making are being, and will be, paid for by the further degradation of the district towards the Strand ... They must then in their turn be scheduled and pulled down'.[131]

In 1896, the Public Health and Housing Committee of the LCC reported of Clare Market and its environs that 'the narrowness, closeness, and bad arrangement and bad condition of the houses, courts, and alleys within the area, and the want of light, air, and ventilation are injurious to the health of the inhabitants'.[132] Booth described houses of three or four storeys sleeping a family in each room and 25 under one roof, with rents per room of 4–5s per week.[133] Because the land was possessed by a large number of small owners, it was agreed that the only way to improve the 'sanitary defects' of the area was an improvement scheme under the Housing of the Working Classes Act (1890). The outcome was the London (Clare Market, Strand) Improvement Scheme of 1895, which proposed to remove all the buildings in the area and replace them with dwellings for 500 people on the same ground, and for a further 1,269 people on the site of the Millbank Penitentiary. These figures were revised after enquiries showed that more than 500 people were employed in the immediate vicinity so would need to be rehoused locally.[134] In the final reckoning, 3,172 people were to be displaced from the Clare Market area, with accommodation for 750 provided on the cleared land and 1,536 in the Millbank Estate, which was completed in 1902.

129 Quoted in *Eighth report of the Medical Officer of the Privy Council (1865)* (Parl. Papers, 1866, XXXIII), Appendix 2, rpt on housing by Dr Julian Hunter, 88.
130 Brownlee, *The Law Courts*, 77; Thornbury, *ONL*, III, 15–25.
131 C. Booth (ed.), *Labour and Life of the People*, II (1891), 296.
132 *Fortieth Annual Report on the Sanitary Condition of the Strand District, London* (1896), 29.
133 LSE, Booth Collection, B340, 23.
134 *Annual report on the statistics and sanitary condition relating to Strand District, London, for the year 1896* (1897), 150; London (Clare Market Strand) Provisional Order Confirmation Act 1897.

Figure 11 *A black and white photo of the old houses on Wych Street, with the spire of St Clement Danes rising above them.*

The problem of overcrowding was exacerbated further, when even more homes were demolished to make space for a road. The newly constituted LCC resurrected the oft-considered scheme for a north–south route between Holborn and the Strand in 1889, citing the need to ease traffic congestion and reduce the stock of insanitary housing.[135] The scheme was put on hold to make provision so that the full cost did not fall on the occupying ratepayer and even as late as 1896, the LCC was criticised for 'their vacillating policy'.[136]

Indecisiveness about implementation of the scheme also delayed any solution to the housing crisis in the area, as another plan to deal with insanitary housing in Clare Market had already been approved by Parliament in 1897.[137] In 1898 the Council was still closing large numbers of properties, displacing around 340 people, most of whom remained living locally. Booth bemoaned local objections to moving further away,

135 LCC, *Opening of Kingsway and Aldwych*, 5.
136 *Reynold's Newspaper*, 24 May 1896.
137 LCC, *Opening of Kingsway and Aldwych*, 8.

claiming: 'The people themselves are the great stumbling block in the way of sanitary progress'.[138] The only accommodation available was vacated by migrating families, who were replaced by poorer residents who rented less space, causing the MOH to warn that 'overcrowding must constantly take place, with deterioration of the property, which is entirely unsuited for the use to which it is now being put'.[139] No space was available for any displaced people, who would have to leave the area or enter the workhouse. This stark choice enhanced the Council's case for rehousing people further from home, where land was significantly cheaper and less built up, so healthier living conditions might be achieved.

To facilitate the construction of Kingsway, around 600 properties were acquired and demolished, freeing up 14 a. of land for new buildings.[140] The block of houses at Holywell Street was removed to widen the Strand and to increase nearby land rents.[141] A tramway subway between Waterloo Bridge and Holborn and memorial statue of Gladstone were included in the plan, which came to an estimated gross cost of £6,120,380.[142]

The Clare Market Improvement Scheme was incorporated into the rebuilding. By 1899, around 1,300 people had been displaced from the Clare Market area, but no replacement homes had been provided.[143] In 1901 the MOH observed that overcrowding had continued to worsen over the previous year.[144] Around 3,700 further people were displaced by the Kingsway and Aldwych development. Edgar Josiah Harper, statistical officer of the LCC told the Joint Select Committee on the Housing of the Working Classes that displaced persons rarely needed to be rehoused in the same area (the law had changed to allow local authorities to rehouse people outside their own area in 1900).[145] Harper argued that the general movement of the population in London meant that it would be better if housing was supplied by a single authority, generally in the suburbs where land was cheaper. His dictum was not universally true. The Strand to Holborn project displaced people with jobs at Covent Garden Market and the theatres, both of which required proximity to their place of employment due to their antisocial hours.[146]

In any case, new occupants moved into the area. The London School of Economics (LSE) obtained a site in Clare Market which was made available by the slum clearances under way. Land was granted by the Technical Education board of the LCC, chaired by LSE founder Sidney Webb. Work began on the Passmore Edwards Hall in 1899 and it was opened by Lord Rosebery, first Chancellor of the University of London, in 1902.[147] Despite the clearances, this was still very much a working neighbourhood, and the school

---

138 LSE, Booth Collection, B340, 7.
139 *Annual report on the Strand District, London, 1898* (1899), 30.
140 LCC, *Opening of Kingsway and Aldwych*, 39.
141 Ibid., 9.
142 Ibid., 12.
143 *Annual report on the Strand District, London, 1899* (1900), 3.
144 *Annual report on the Strand District, London, 1900* (1901), 3.
145 S. Durgan, 'Leading the way: council housing in Westminster', *Westminster Hist. Rev.*, 3 (2000), 27.
146 *Report from the Joint Select Committee of the House of Lords and the House of Commons on Housing of the Working Classes; together with the proceedings of the committee, minutes of evidence, appendix and index* (Parl. Papers, 1902 (325) v), p. 115.
147 J. Beveridge, *An Epic of Clare Market: Birth and early days of the London School of Economics* (1960), 45–7.

was surrounded by the noise of the St Clement's Press, two public houses and several organ grinders.[148]

The *Illustrated London News* ran a feature entitled 'Destroyed by improvements: where Aldwych and Kingsway stand', with pictures of the particularly old buildings that had been knocked down in Butchers' Row, Wych Street and Holywell Street. These were the largest collection of buildings remaining in London from before the Great Fire. Not only were they of historical value, these areas had been in reasonably good condition and were classified on Booth's poverty map of 1898–99 as 'fairly comfortable' or 'well-to-do'.[149]

148 Ibid., 58.
149 https://booth.lse.ac.uk/map (accessed 5 Nov. 2016).

ECONOMIC HISTORY

DURING THE LATE 16TH AND early 17th century, the parish exhibited an 'extreme social pattern' of gentlemen and servants, with few other occupational groups present in significant numbers, although it was already part of the legal quarter of London.[1] It was both fairly rich and, without any large parks, leafy suburbs or unbuilt-on land, densely populated. In the 17th century, land in St Clement Danes had a relatively high value of £1,936/ha, but lower than the commercial centres of Westminster in parts of St Martin-in-the-Fields, and far less than the £5,699/ha. in the neighbourhood of the Royal Exchange and Cornhill, at the heart of the City.[2] Mean household rent was just above the Westminster average of £21 14s per annum.[3] Using a stock valuation assessment (measuring net wealth deemed to be the source of the assessed person's income), the north-east part of St Clement Danes had a mean stock value of £160 17s., with some of the western section over £100 higher. The part of the parish north of St Clement Danes Church, around Clement's Inn, had a lowly mean stock value of £71 3s., while the parish mean was £132 4s. The Westminster mean was around £180.[4] Levels of poverty in the parish were very low. In 1664 only 3.4 per cent of households in the parish were exempt from paying the rates due to poverty. In Westminster and the West End, the average was 28.5 per cent.[5] Nevertheless, parishioners appear to have been highly resistant to paying the hearth tax, as 42 per cent of households did not pay in 1666.[6]

Although there is little occupational data for this early period, the removal of the aristocratic houses by the Strand and their replacement with rows of desirable but more manageably sized houses facilitated growth in the number of professionals in the parish, particularly lawyers. Admissions to the Inns of Court were at a higher number during both decades between 1680 and 1699 than in any decade in the 18th century, which must have increased the presence of lawyers in the area.[7] A misogynist jibe of 1728 shows that the parish was deeply associated with the legal profession, which was an avenue for social advancement but also a source of ridicule: 'The Parishioners of St. Clement Danes would

1   A.L. Beier, 'Engine of manufacture: the trades of London', in A.L. Beier and R. Finlay (eds), *London 1500–1700: The Making of the Metropolis* (1986), 155; M.J. Power, 'The social Topography of Restoration London', in A.L. Beier and R. Finlay (eds), *London 1500–1700*, 202.
2   Spence, *London in the 1690s*, 51–2.
3   Ibid., 176–8.
4   Ibid., 149–56.
5   J. Boulton, 'The poor among the rich: paupers and the parish in the West End, 1600–1724', in P. Griffiths and M.S.R. Jenner (eds), *Londinopolis: Essays in the Cultural and Social History of Early Modern London* (Manchester and New York, 2000), 209.
6   Davies et al (eds), *London and Middlesex 1666 Hearth Tax*, 71–6, 92, 312.
7   P. Lucas, 'A collective biography of students and barristers of Lincoln's Inn, 1680–1804: a study in the "aristocratic resurgence" of the eighteenth century', *Jnl of Modern History*, 46:2 (1974), 245–6.

feign appear more polite than their Neighbours, by breeding up their Sons, and sometimes even their Daughters to practise the Law.[8] Other occupations in the parish become easier to enumerate over time, but in all periods the majority of people would have worked in occupations such as domestic service or labouring. Intermittent poverty meant that many would have slipped in and out of the black economy. The section of the Strand between Temple Bar and Exeter Exchange was particularly notorious for prostitutes, pickpockets and general criminality.[9] Nevertheless St Clement Danes still had a relatively high proportion of households (53.5 per cent) in the top two of five tax brackets in 1798, much higher than the 5.9 per cent in the poorest London parish of Bermondsey, but well below the richest, Bread Street, with 79.8 per cent.[10]

The Westminster poll books of the late 18th and early 19th century contained the name, address, votes and also the occupation of voters. This occupational data can be used to create a partial picture of the economic life of the parish, representing those able to take part in the formal political process and who would have dominated the open vestry. This data provides an idea of the geography of occupations in the parish. It should be borne in mind that this is a very select group of adult, male ratepayers, comprising only the wealthiest 15 to 20 per cent of men, or one in four of the adult male workforce.[11] St Clement Danes was included in a voting district with the neighbouring parish of St Mary-le-Strand, but using the combined data it is possible to see how a section of occupations in the parish changed over time. Some occupations also show clear geographic clustering. Occupational data has been analysed from the poll books for the Westminster elections of 1749 and 1818.[12]

	St Clement Danes	Per cent of total	Westminster	Per cent of total
Agriculture	0	0	141	2
Building	55	6	884	9
Dealing	325	37	2975	32
Domestic service	5	1	163	2
Industrial service	1	0	123	1
Manufacturing	333	37	3015	32
Public service/ Professional	29	3	388	4
Rentiers	130	15	1541	16
Transport	6	1	207	2
Total	884		9437	

Table 1 *Occupational data from the 1749 Westminster poll book for St Clement Danes and St Mary-le-Strand, compiled and categorised by the* Westminster Historical Database.

8   E. Jones, *A trip through London: containing observations on men and things. To which is added, a brief and merry character of Ireland, by a Berkshire gentleman lately return'd from that kingdom. The third edition with additions* (1728), 36.

9   T. Henderson, *Disorderly Women in Eighteenth-Century London: prostitution and control in the metropolis, 1730–1830* (1999), 59.

10   L.D. Schwarz, 'Social class and social geography: the middle classes in London at the end of the eighteenth century', *Social History*, 7:2 (1982), 183.

11   Methodology from 'St Clement Danes', *LL*, and C.E. Harvey, E.M. Green and P.J. Corfield, 'Continuity, change, and specialisation within metropolitan London: the economy of Westminster, 1750–1820', *Econ. Hist. Rev.*, 52, 2 (1999), 490.

12   C.E. Harvey, E.M. Green and P.J. Corfield, *The Westminster Historical Database: Voters, social structure and electoral behaviour* (Bristol, 1998).

Figure 12 *This satirical print shows a fop, based on Garrick's character Fribble from a recent play, hung from a hook by the butchers of Clare Market.*

By far the two largest occupational groups in St Clement Danes and St Mary-le-Strand in 1749 were manufacturing (333) and dealing (325), although the division between these categories is deeply problematic, as in reality many artisans also sold their own wares. Nevertheless, the proportion of both groups was significantly larger than for Westminster as a whole, confirming the commercial character of parish householders. The largest sectors within manufacturing were dress (181), including 122 tailors, and dress sundries (32). The area sandwiched between Drury Lane and Clare Market had a high concentration of manufacturers; tailors in particular were found in smaller groupings there, with 13 in Stanhope Street, 12 in White Horse Yard, seven in Holywell Street and six in Craven Buildings.

The biggest groups included in dealing were food sellers (118), and vendors of wines, spirits and hoteliers (88). Forty-five butchers were to be found in Clare Market from a total of 67. The market itself supported an ecosystem of 17 other food dealers, such as cheesemongers or victuallers and dozens more in the close surroundings such as Clare Street, Holles Street and Vere Street. Francis Place wrote a vivid description of his father's tavern, the King's Head in Arundel Street around 1780, which had a tap room, a parlour where many neighbours gathered, and two club rooms where a punch club drank until drunk, usually between midnight and two o'clock in the morning, on Mondays and

Fridays.[13] Other leisure facilities included a cold bath on Surrey Street which proudly advertised its use by inhabitants of the Inns of Court in 1778 and could still be visited from Strand Lane in 2018.[14] Rentiers have been divided into 115 gentlemen and 15 esquires, although most of these were in fact lawyers; 76 of the gentlemen were in the three Inns of Chancery in St Clement Danes. These were men such as Charles Massey of Clement's Inn, deputy to the solicitor for the affairs of the admiralty and Richard Fisher of Lyon's Inn, a conveyancer.[15] A large proportion of the builders were carpenters (24).

	St Clement Danes	Per cent of total	Westminster	Per cent of total
Agriculture	5	0	75	1
Building	77	6	821	8
Dealing	427	35	3482	35
Domestic service	22	2	181	2
Industrial service	10	1	180	2
Manufacturing	338	28	3178	31
Public service/ Professional	237	19	739	7
Rentiers	92	8	1286	13
Transport	8	1	150	1
Total	1216		10092	

Table 2 *Occupational data from the 1818 Westminster poll book for St Clement Danes and St Mary-le-Strand, compiled and categorised by the* Westminster Historical Database.

Comparison can be made with occupations in the poll book of 1818, although changes in numbers of an occupation only show that not as many qualified as voters, so describe a combination of change in economic fortunes as well as absolute growth or decline. By 1818, dealing (427) had overtaken manufacturing (338) as the largest occupational group and the latter had fallen below the percentage in Westminster as a whole. The number of food sellers declined to 110, with the number of butchers almost halving to 36 and only 11 remaining in Clare Market, confirming its decline in fortunes. Vendors of wines, spirits and hoteliers also declined in number slightly to 83. Growth in the dealing sector clearly came about through greater diversity, with six categories from coal sellers to general dealers numbering in their twenties or thirties. Stationers (including booksellers) enjoyed the biggest increase in the dealing sector, from seven to 42. Five booksellers had shops on the fashionable Strand whilst law stationers stayed close to the Inns of Court, with five based on Carey Street alone.

Dress accounted for only 131 people in 1818, the number of tailors falling to 65. The shift from manufacturing to dealing was apparent in White Horse Yard, where a single

13   Thale (ed.), *The Autobiography of Francis Place*, 37–40.
14   M. Trapp, 'The Georgian History of the Strand Lane 'Roman' Bath', *The London Journal*, 39:2 (2014), 152.
15   *LL*, City of London Sess.: Sess. papers – justices' working docs, 12 Sept. 1749, LMSLPS150600033 (accessed 6 June 2017); *London Evening Post*, 5–8 May 1753.

woollen draper of 1749 was replaced by nine in 1818, but only two tailors remained. The movement of richer tailors out of the parish is typified by Francis Place, who relocated to Charing Cross in 1799 to establish a fashionable shop with window displays, greatly increasing his customer base and profitability.[16] Manufacturers of dress sundries fell drastically in number to seven, with the number of peruke makers collapsing from 29 to none, due to changing fashions. Distilling also collapsed, from 19 to none.

Holywell Street provides a complex picture of the changing numbers of manufacturers and dealers in dress. The seven tailors and a single stocking maker in 1749 made way for an expanded 12 manufacturers of dress or dress sundries, with only three tailors, but more specialists such as a robe maker and two stay makers. Dealers in clothing material or dress seemingly collapsed from ten, mostly mercers and drapers, to five, including four silk merchants and a clothes dealer. These may be accounted for by the appearance of ten 'salesmen', likely members of the second-hand clothes trade that overtook the street in the early 19th century, so that by 1842 it was described in a story as 'a sort of national gallery of cast-off clothes'.[17] The story had an anti-Semitic tone, but did identify a genuine Jewish community: three of the Holywell Street salesmen listed in the poll book were called E. Gompertz, Moses Levy and Joseph Levy. The Jewish community here increased in numbers and was increasingly subjected to stereotyping and insults as the 19th century wore on.[18]

Many other sectors pushed past manufacturing of dress sundries, the largest of which were printers (44), gold, silver and jewel workers (26), furniture makers (22), bakers (19), tool makers (15) and woodworkers (14). There was an overall shift away from the essentials of dress to the manufacture of more luxury goods, such as books and jewellery. There was a seedier side to the growth in printers and booksellers, as Holywell Street became notorious for the production and sale of pornography, attracting proprietors such as the radical-turned-pornographer William Dugdale.[19] In other sectors, the largest group amongst the 77 builders were still carpenters (30). The increase in domestic service from five to 22 was explained by a few more cooks and servants, as well as the replacement of one barber by ten hairdressers. This picture of a growing service economy and increasing specialisation reflects how 'London's role at the heart of interlocking regional, national, and international networks became ever more crucial and, simultaneously, diversified'.[20]

The largest increase was in the public service/professional sector, which leapt from only 3 per cent of the total in 1749 to 19 per cent in 1818. While the parishes seemingly hosted only three legal professionals in 1749, by 1818 there were 184, accounting for most of the increase in public service/professional workers. Of those 184, the major categories were 84 solicitors, 59 attorneys and 33 barristers. Much of the meteoric rise in the legal profession can be explained by a change of designation from rentiers. In 1749 legal professionals who aspired to respectability classified themselves as gentlemen or esquires.[21] By 1818, the three Inns accounted for 27 gentlemen and 46 legal professionals.

16   Thale (ed.), *The Autobiography of Francis Place*, 201.
17   *Brother Jonathan* (New York, 1842), 98.
18   Nead, *Victorian Babylon*, 174–7.
19   Ibid., 178; McCalman, 'Unrespectable radicalism', 77.
20   Harvey, Green and Corfield, "Continuity, change, and specialisation', 478.
21   P.J. Corfield, *Power and the Professions in Britain 1700–1850* (2012), 80.

Figure 13 *Boswell Court, shortly before its demolition to clear the way for the Royal Courts of Justice.*

Lincoln's Inn accounted for one gentleman and 58 legal professionals in 1818, following the inclusion of part of its area in this electoral division. Most of the remaining legal professionals resided on the streets closest to Lincoln's Inn, such as Serle Street, Carey Street and Boswell Court. In contrast, the 14 medical professionals of 1749, who made up a majority of the category at the time, had only swelled their ranks to 19 by 1818. Lucrative government posts were now available, with 14 navy agents based in Clement's and New Inns or streets south of the Strand, and four sheriff's officers present in 1818. Three artists were also a new addition.

The 1851 census gives a more complete picture of employment in the parish.[22] Women were predominantly employed in domestic services (29 per cent), textiles (21 per cent), and other services, mostly charwomen and laundry workers (16 per cent). Of the individual occupation groups that were predominantly female the most frequent

22   All occupation figures from the census are for those aged 14 years and older to exclude children, most of
     whom were at school or had no occupation listed.

were, in descending order, domestic servants (by far the largest single category), laundry workers, dressmakers, shirt makers and seamstresses, charwomen, and wives or others with household duties. The occupations open to women had changed little since the 18th century.[23]

Men were employed in a greater spread of occupations, including textiles: dress (11 per cent), conveyance including porterage (9 per cent), print and books (8 per cent), housebuilding (7 per cent), and food (7 per cent). The most frequent masculine occupations were messengers or porters or watchmen, tailors, shoe and boot makers, general labourers, commercial or business clerks, carpenters or joiners, printers, domestic servants, stationers and butchers. These occupations reflect the unique London labour market, which had much higher percentages of men working in the transport and service sectors than the rest of England.[24] Although not directly comparable to figures compiled by Schwarz for the whole of London due to differences in categorisation, it is still clear that St Clement Danes had remarkably high numbers of printers and lawyers compared to the rest of the city.[25] Occupations with greater balance between the sexes included bookbinders (more women than men), shoe and boot makers (more men than women), and of private means (slightly more men).

Several trades including domestic servants, and the 'charwomen, caretakers, costers, porters etc.' still resident in Clare Market in 1899, were typical of the casual and poor workers who needed to live within walking distance of their place of work and might be constantly on call.[26] The number of women working in dress manufacture was greater than the number of men, reflecting patterns in the east of London and suggesting sweated domestic labour supplying wholesale 'slop shops', rather than the vote-holding artisan tailors identified in the poll books just over 30 years previously.[27] These changes should not be overstated as the 18th-century workforce undoubtedly struggled for a decent living and in the case of tailors were 'generally as poor as Rats'.[28]

The details of two parish families recorded in the 1851 census help to illustrate the contrasting living arrangements and disparities in wealth present in the parish. The Millers of 32 Essex Street had a household of 14 people. Head of the family, Robert Miller, born in Ireland, was a 53 year old serjeant at law who lived with his 45 year old wife Jane. They had two adult sons, one was a barrister and the other an undergraduate at Oxford. They had another three sons and a daughter, all at school, and a one year old son. Also part of the household were four female servants ranging from between 21 and 48 years old (one Irish, one from Salisbury, Wiltshire, and two Londoners) and a male servant aged 19 years from Buckinghamshire. Another family, also with an Irish head of household, provides a striking comparison. The seven Shaws of 9 Ship Yard, which was cleared away to build the Royal Courts of Justice, were headed by matriarch Ellen,

23 L.D. Schwarz, *London in the Age of Industrialisation: Entrepreneurs, Labour Force and Living Conditions, 1700–1850* (Cambridge, 1992), 19.

24 Ibid., 23.

25 Ibid., 42.

26 LSE, Booth Collection, B244, 199; G. Stedman Jones, *Outcast London: A Study in the Relationship Between Classes in Victorian Society* (Oxford, 1971), 171.

27 Green, *From Artisans to Paupers*, 163–8.

28 Schwarz, *London in the Age of Industrialisation*, 180–1; R. Campbell, *The London Tradesman: Being a Compendious View of All the Trades, Professions, Arts, Both Liberal and Mechanic, Now Practised in the Cities of London and Westminster* (1747), 193.

a 59 year old charwoman. The rest of her family were born in St Clement Danes. She lived with her three sons, all cabmen, aged between 30 and 35, and her daughter, also Ellen, who was 25 and a servant. Ellen Senior's two granddaughters also lived there; one was only nine months old, but 12 year old Mary Ann was expected to pay her way and worked as a servant. The Shaws shared their address with 18 other people.

Between 1851 and 1901 there were small falls in the percentage of people engaged in almost all industrial and manufacturing related activities, and small rises in service industries and the book and stationary trade. Although the category of professionals increased overall, there were more nurses but fewer lawyers. The largest rise of 4 per cent was in people providing food and lodging, with a particularly large rise in the number of barmen, a notoriously youthful occupation with a tendency, according to Charles Booth, to become loafers.[29] Booth also named flower sellers and street porters in the occupations of people living and sleeping 'like animals' in conditions 'too disgusting for words' in the streets and lanes off the Strand.[30] The major change was a huge fall in people working or dealing in dress, from 15 to five per cent. All of the individual occupations mentioned above in this category, from tailors to shoe makers, fell sharply in numbers. Booth noted that the large fall in population in the Strand district between 1861 and 1891 was mostly due to the removal of dwellings and their replacement by warehouses and business premises, meaning large numbers of people came to work in the area for the day.[31] Nevertheless, slum clearance clearly had a dramatic effect on the occupational structure of the remaining residents in the parish.

The Twinings

The Twining family and their business interests provide a case study of the upper echelons of the economic life in the parish across almost the entire period. Consistently successful and civically active, the Twinings can fairly be described as a St Clement Danes dynasty.[32] Thomas Twining (1675–1741) was an apprentice to an East India merchant, and then around 1706, he became proprietor of Tom's Coffee House in Devereux Court, a single block away from the parish church. Fulfilling his duty in parish politics, he was an overseer of the poor in 1714–15.[33] Thomas was more focussed on the tea trade than his coffee house, which he sublet around 1734.[34] The family business passed to Daniel Twining (1713–62) who became a partner in 1734 and whose widow, Mary, took over its running at his death. Daniel may have been rich enough to pay a fine to avoid parochial office, but was happy to help examine the parish organ and assess the need for repairs.[35]

29   Stedman Jones, *Outcast London*, 70.
30   LSE, Booth Collection, B340, 13.
31   LSE, Booth Collection, B340, 3.
32   *ODNB*, s.v., Twining, Richard (1749–1824), tea and coffee merchant (accessed 18 Feb. 2014).
33   WCA, St CD Vestry Mins, B1062, 22 July 1714.
34   S.H. Twining, *House of Twining* (1956), 12.
35   WCA, St CD Vestry Mins, B1067, 9 Apr. 1747, 28 Sept. 1747.

Figure 14 *The Twinings tea shop, still at 216 Strand as of 2018.*

Their son Richard (1749–1824) was born in Devereux Court and left Eton College in 1763 to help his mother, eventually taking over the firm in 1771.[36] Richard became Chairman of the trade body for dealers of tea, a director of the East India Company and advised William Pitt to reduce tax on the commodity. Under his guidance the business expanded, opening an entrance at 216 Strand in 1787. He had five sons and three daughters. The eldest son, Richard Twining II (1772–1857), was also born in Devereux Court and joined the family business at the age of fifteen. He became a partner, as did his brothers George and John, the three of them taking over in 1818.

In the febrile years of the French Revolution and Napoleonic Wars the family busied themselves with local initiatives in support of their king and country. The parish Loyalist Association established in 1792 was chaired by John Twining, with Richard Twining also sitting on the committee.[37] The parish Voluntary Armed Association had both Richard Twining senior and junior on its committee, three of the family becoming lieutenants or higher.[38] In 1825, with the three Twining brothers in charge, the business expanded

36   Twining, *House of Twining*, 43.
37   *World (1787)*, 13 Dec. 1792.
38   *True Briton (1793)*, 5 May 1798.

into banking and they built a new banking house on the Strand in 1835. The bank was amalgamated with Lloyds in 1892, where Richard Twining III became a director. Richard II was hugely involved in the life of St Clement Danes, serving on the vestry, on the management committee of King's College Hospital and, as chairman of the trustees of the Holborn Estate Charity, laid the foundation stone for almshouses in Tooting.[39] His two daughters, Elizabeth (1805–89) and Louisa (1820–1912) both remained unmarried and devoted themselves to philanthropic works. Elizabeth set up and managed a temperance hall in Portugal Street.[40]

The eldest son of Richard Twining II, Richard III (1807–1906), became a partner in the firm in 1829. In 1837 the company was granted a Royal Warrant and the Devereux Court premises were rebuilt and extended in 1843–4. Richard III took over the business with his cousin in 1857. Also active in local affairs, he was a president of King's College Hospital and a Justice of the Peace for Westminster.[41] He declined to stand as an MP for Westminster in 1865, instead recruiting another local businessman, the stationer and bookseller W.H. Smith, who represented Westminster and later the Strand district from 1868–91.[42] Richard Twining III and his cousin retired in 1897, after partially rebuilding the Devereux Court premises again in 1893, and passed the business on to a sixth generation of the family. Other 19th-century family members included Herbert Haynes Twining, a vestryman then councillor and Samuel Twining who was a churchwarden. In 2018, the Strand site is still occupied by a Twinings tea shop and museum. Stephen Twining, a tenth generation family member, worked as a global ambassador for the company.[43]

Theatres

The theatres based in the parish were part of the cluster around nearby Covent Garden while the Strand, at least until the middle of the 19th century, 'was the centre of press, printsellers and establishments for entertainment'.[44] Theatres returned to St Clement Danes soon after the restoration in 1660, having been suppressed during the interregnum. Thomas Killigrew, one of the two holders of a patent to stage plays granted by Charles II, followed the French model of converting an indoor tennis court to a theatre in Vere Street in 1660, although he soon moved to the purpose-built Theatre Royal.[45] The Duke's Company, led by William Davenant, converted another old tennis court just south of Lincoln's Inn Fields into a theatre in 1661, where they remained until 1671. This was apparently the first theatre to witness the innovation of female roles being

39   M. Anson, *The St Clement Danes Holborn Estate Charity, the first 450 years* (2004), 17.
40   *ODNB*, s.v., Twining, Elizabeth (1805–1889), botanic artist and social reformer (accessed 18 Feb. 2014).
41   Twining, *House of Twining*, 74; R.J.B. Pooley, *The History of St Clement Danes Holborn Estate Grammar School* (no date), 35.
42   M. Baer, *The Rise and Fall of Radical Westminster, 1780–1890* (2012), 214.
43   'History of Twinings', http://www.twinings.co.uk/about-twinings/history-of-twinings (accessed 17 May 2017).
44   Baer, *Radical Westminster*, 222.
45   G. Bush-Bailey, *Treading the Bawds: Actresses and playwrights on the late-Stuart stage* (Manchester, 2006), 27.

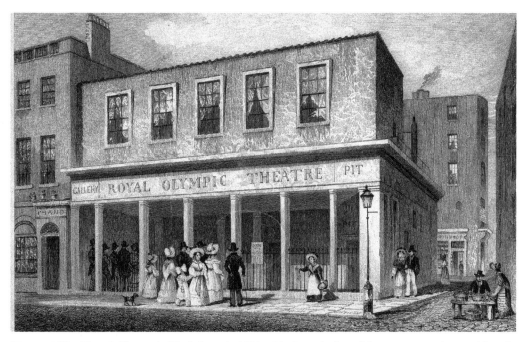

Figure 15 *The Olympic Theatre in Wych Street in 1831, with elegantly dressed figures congregating outside and a street seller at his stall.*

played by women.[46] The King's Company used the theatre from 1672 to 1674, when it reverted back to use as a tennis court. The theatre was revived by a breakaway group headed by leading actor Thomas Betterton in 1695.[47] It was rebuilt in 1714 and used sporadically until 1744.[48] One of its most noted productions was John Gay's *Beggar's Opera*, which debuted there in 1727 and enjoyed a run of 63 consecutive performances.[49] The area also attracted other less reputable artists; the rate books for 1668 show that Portugal Street was home to some wealthy and notable residents, including poet and libertine John Wilmot, 2nd earl of Rochester (d. 1680).[50]

Another of the parish's most noted theatres, the Lyceum started out as an exhibition and concert hall, designed by James Paine in 1765. It was converted for use as a theatre by owner Dr Samuel Arnold in 1794. He was unable to obtain a license to present drama and so it was let by the New Circus. In the 1790s the building passed into the hands of the owner's son, S.J. Arnold and was renamed the Lyceum Theatre. In 1802 it hosted Madame Tussaud's first waxwork exhibition in Britain. Drama at the theatre only really picked up in 1809, when the Theatre Royal, Drury Lane burned down and its company moved temporarily to the Lyceum. Following their departure in 1812, it was used mainly for opera and was rebuilt as the Theatre Royal English Opera House in 1816.

46   Diprose, *Some Account*, 76–7.
47   C. Cibber, *An Apology for the Life of Mr. Colley Cibber, Comedian, and Late Patentee of the Theatre-Royal* (1740), 158; J. Milhous, *Thomas Betterton and the Management of Lincoln's Inn Fields, 1695–1708* (Illinois, 1979), ch. 3.
48   M. Banham (ed.), *The Cambridge Guide to Theatre* (Cambridge, 1995), 643.
49   Diprose, *Some Account*, 77.
50   Thornbury, *ONL, III,* 26–32.

The new building itself burned down in 1830 and was rebuilt a little to the west, four years later. The Covent Garden Theatre Company took over in 1856, after their theatre also burnt down. Henry Irving became actor-manager in 1878 and sustained the theatre into the 20th century with his wife and leading lady, Ellen Terry.[51] The Lyceum was joined in the 19th century by the Olympic Theatre on Wych Street, which opened in 1806 on the site of Craven House and was rebuilt following a fire in 1840.[52] The Strand Theatre occupied the building of Burford's Panoramas, west of Norfolk Street, and opened in 1832.[53] Both were demolished for the building of Aldwych in 1904.[54]

The taverns around Clare Market provided a thriving social scene for those connected to the theatre, along with other artists. The Bull's Head Tavern hosted a club of artists, authors and actors, many connected to the Lincoln's Inn Fields Theatre. Its members included Colley Cibber, Tom D'Urfey and William Hogarth.[55] The nearby Black Jack was the favoured haunt of comedian Joe Miller. Upon his death in 1738 he was buried in the parish graveyard in Portugal Street, where many other actors were interred. The same tavern hosted a club called the Honourable Society of Jackers, which included many popular actors, including John Kemble and John Pritt Harley, until it ceased to meet in 1816.[56]

Theatre culture was by no means exclusive and it permeated the wider community. The butchers of Clare Market were notorious for their vocal role in the nearby theatres, passing judgement on plays, attending the funerals of actors and leading the occasional mob in theatrical rows. Some theatre managers even quoted the butchers' approval in their advertisements.[57] A Clare Market butcher was apparently the author of an epitaph on the actor James Spiller, calling for his fellow butchers to lay down their marrow bones and cleavers and pray for Spiller. It also urged the butchers to pay a subscription for an engraving of Spiller and, although it was probably never produced, a likeness of him did replace the sign for the aforementioned Bull's Head Tavern, converting it to the Spiller's Head.[58] The parish also had a role to play in 'the last great theatre riot in English history', the Old Price Riots surrounding Covent Garden Theatre in 1809. Opposition to price rises in the newly rebuilt theatre was co-ordinated by a committee that met in the Crown and Anchor tavern, Strand.[59]

51   M. Kilburn, *London's Theatres* (2011), 77–8.
52   *Universal Mag.* (Nov. 1806), 435; *View of part of Craven House in Wych Street. The Site of the Olympic Theatre* (1822), BM; *View of the first Olympic Theatre, or Olympic Pavilion* (1805) BM; *The Olympic Theatre, Wych-Street, Strand, Destroyed by Fire, on Thursday, March 29* (1849), BM; T. Hosmer Shepherd, *View of the Royal Olympic Theatre* (1849), BM.
53   *Morning Post*, 25 Jan. 1832.
54   Banham (ed.), *The Cambridge Guide to Theatre*, 819.
55   S. Ireland, *Graphic Illustrations of Hogarth* (1794), 77; *London Literary Gaz.*, 22 Sept. 1821.
56   J. Timbs, *Club life of London with anecdotes of the clubs, coffee houses and taverns of the metropolis during the 17th, 18th and 19th centuries*, II (1866), 184–5.
57   Thornbury, *ONL*, III, 36–44.
58   Ireland, *Graphic Illustrations of Hogarth*, 76–7.
59   M. Baer, *Theatre and Disorder in Late Georgian London* (Oxford, 1992), 1, 145.

Figure 16 *Samuel Johnson and Boswell dining at a chop house. Although it is not specifically set in the parish, it is no stretch to suggest that it could have been.*

Literary Life

The vibrant literary life in St Clement Danes had an influence on the character of the parish beyond its undoubted economic importance. Arundel House was used as a meeting place by the Royal Society following the Great Fire, while the newly flourishing coffee houses offered more informal venues.[60] The Grecian coffee house in Devereux Court was often frequented by members of the Royal Society, including the astronomer Edmond Halley, the physicist Sir Isaac Newton and the physician and collector Sir Hans Sloane. The Grecian was renowned for hosting learned conversation rather than gossip.[61]

The Crown and Anchor tavern, located opposite St Clement Danes Church, was an important public venue in 18th and 19th-century London, hosting many notable political meetings and a diverse range of cultural and professional associations, including the Royal Society and the British Medical Association, and was the birthplace of the Academy of Musicians, which counted George Frederick Handel as a founding member.[62] The tavern also hosted lectures by literary figures such as Coleridge and Hazlitt.[63] It was renovated and expanded in 1787 to stretch an entire block from Arundel Street to Milford Lane, although with various shops and other buildings separating it from the Strand. The large dining room could host upwards of 500 people, while the Great Assembly Room was one of the largest rooms available for hire in London, with

60   Evelyn, *Diary and Correspondence*, II, 20 and 89.
61   Phillips, *Mid-Georgian London*, 183.
62   *London Chronicle*, 28 Nov. 1789; *The Times*, 1 Dec. 1831; R. Elkin, *The Old Concert Rooms of London* (London, 1955), 50–7.
63   P.J. Manning, 'Manufacturing the Romantic image: Hazlitt and Coleridge lecturing', in J. Chandler and K. Gilmartin (eds.), *Romantic Metropolis: The urban Scene of British Culture, 1780–1840* (Cambridge, 2003), 227–45.

a capacity of around 2,000. These were supplemented by numerous smaller meeting rooms, as well as a drawing room, smoking room, library and a ladies room.[64]

The most famed literary figure with strong connections to St Clement Danes was Samuel Johnson. His provincial birth perhaps gives him an even greater claim to being an archetypal parishioner and Londoner. In all the years he lived in London, Johnson lodged for the most part, either in or near the parish, amongst the printers and publishers clustered in the area.[65] He favoured the church of St Clement Danes, which catered to his High Anglican leanings and he put his charitable instincts to work helping the numerous poor people he lived near to.[66] Many of Boswell's anecdotes about Johnson were based in taverns and coffee houses in this part of London, where he revelled in literary sociability to complement his solitary endeavour.[67] To give examples of his many haunts, the St Clement Danes Chop House and Clifton's Chop House on Butchers' Row were mentioned many times by Boswell in his diary of 1762–3.[68] Johnson founded a convivial dining club in the Essex Head tavern on Essex Street just a year before his death, which was continued by the 'clubbable' Boswell for many years afterwards.[69] In 1851 the parishioners paid for an inscription on the pew where Johnson supposedly sat and a statue erected of him outside the church in 1910 still stood there in 2018.[70]

64   C. Parolin, *Radical Spaces: Venues of Popular Politics in London, c.1790–1845* (Canberra, 2010), 111–2.
65   J. Boswell, *The Life of Samuel Johnson*, III (1820), 457.
66   Boswell, *The Life of Samuel Johnson*, II (1820), 218; III (1820), 12, 428.
67   e.g., Boswell, *The Life of Samuel Johnson*, II (1820), 49, 186, 191 and 473.
68   J. Boswell, *London Jnl 1762–1763* (2010), e.g. 190, 194, 217, 265, 292.
69   Boswell, *The Life of Samuel Johnson*, IV (1820), 271–3, 275, 295 and 376; Timbs, *Club Life of London*, I, 202–4.
70   Thornbury, *ONL*, III, 10–15; *The Times*, 5 Aug. 1910.

LOCAL GOVERNMENT

Parochial Government

PERHAPS UNSURPRISINGLY GIVEN ITS COMPLEX composition, the exact delineation
of local government powers in Westminster was never entirely settled, even with
the creation of the Court of Burgesses and a City government in 1585.[1] By the later
17th century, however, it becomes possible to sketch out the basic parameters of
local government in St Clement Danes, and to chart the impact of various pieces of
Parliamentary legislation, local acts, and locally relevant events, on the functions and
functioning of vestry government in the parish.

A handful of parochial sources exist for the late 16th and first half of the 17th
century,[2] but the earliest extant material relating to parish government is contained in
the volumes of vestry minutes which commence in 1668. The first volume, covering the
period between April 1668 and December 1677, has suffered significant water damage,
and the second, covering the period between 1678 and 1686, was unfortunately destroyed
during the Second World War. This series of volumes, alongside various Parliamentary
acts, the minutes of the Court of Burgesses (itself missing volumes covering the period
1615 to 1705) and the records of the court leet of the Duchy Liberty, identifies the main
features of vestry government from the 17th century onwards.

The Later 17th Century

As with most other English parishes, the vestry was the cornerstone of local government
in St Clement Danes. Prior to the early 19th century, English parishes were bodies that
operated under a mass of different rules, regulations and remits, many particular to a
single parish. As a consequence, their spheres of activity could extend into a variety of
areas of parochial life that the vestry was prepared and able to engage in. There were,
however, several core services that Westminster parishes such as St Clement Danes were
expected to deliver – poor relief, policing, and street maintenance and cleaning – and
that generated the great majority of vestry business. These services were, to some degree
or other, paid for by various rates levied on householders in the parish. The rates were
also highly significant in the context of parochial government, as only those who paid

---

1 G. Rosser, *Medieval Westminster: 1200–1540* (Oxford, 1989) 226–48; *VCH Middx* XIII, 4–8; J. Merritt, *The Social World of Early Modern Westminster* (Manchester, 2005), 225–56.

2 These consist of records relating to the Poor Law: Overseers' accounts, 1604–1900; settlement papers and removal orders, 1645; bastardy bonds, registers, 1641; apprenticeship indentures and registers, 1640–1711; along with papers relating to Highways and Health, 1581–1855, and surveyors accounts, 1581–1704.

Figure 17 *The view looking east across London from Arundel House, from an etching by Wenceslaus Hollar. The artist's position is not far from that taken up for a painting of the Embankment around 200 years later (see fig. 2).*

them – those who were rateable – were eligible to vote and be a constituent part of the vestry.

If they were 'open', these gatherings of parochial inhabitants for the purposes of administration and decision making could be attended by any householder: the head of the household eligible for assessment for parish rates. There were approximately 1,729 householders in the parish in 1708.[3] In the late 17th century, however, the vestry of St Clement Danes, like a number in Westminster, was 'select' or 'close', meaning only a limited number of householders were able to attend vestry meetings. In practice this meant that all parochial authority was vested in a small group of men – the 'ancients' or 'principal inhabitants' of the parish, as they often styled themselves – who formed an exclusive and self-perpetuating oligarchy. Whether the St Clement Danes vestry had always been select is not clear, although the earliest recorded vestry meetings in the late 1660s barely comprised more than a dozen men.[4] The close vestry of St Clement Danes seems to have based its claim to authority on immemorial custom, with the rector and some of the other inhabitants assuming the right to select the vestrymen.[5] The same small clique also appointed men to fill parish offices.[6]

The vestry met in a public room called the vestry room or church house at the east end of the parish churchyard, as and when required.[7] The building was rebuilt

3   Hatton, *London*, I, 207.
4   WCA, St CD Vestry Mins, B1058, 1668–1677, B1060, 1686–1699.
5   WCA, St CD Vestry Mins, B1061, 30 Dec. 1700; B. and S. Webb, *English Local Government: the parish and the county* (1906), 175–90.
6   Bodl. Rawlinson B. 377, 27 Mar. 1701, f. 2.
7   Ibid.

by the vestry on the orders of the Middlesex justices in the 1650s, as the structure had apparently become ruinous. It was also used as a meeting house for the Court of Burgesses and court leet of the Duchy Liberty, and was therefore also known as the Duchy office in the Strand. The ground floor of the building served as an almshouse with six rooms. The floor above consisted of two rooms. The larger room to the north – the courthouse – contained a bar for the court itself and was adorned with the king's arms. The smaller southern room was the preserve of the burgesses, and contained the records of the burgess court of the Duchy Liberty. This room also acted as a 'withdrawal room' for the various parochial and manorial juries, and as a storehouse for the parish plate, linen and arms for the Duchy Liberty's militia.[8]

April meetings to select the churchwardens for the ensuing year were a fixture in the calendar by the 1690s.[9] The incumbent or rector of St Clement Danes parish church was an ex-officio member of the vestry until the Local Government Act of 1899, and had the right to chair vestry meetings until the Local Government Act of 1894.[10] Despite his right to chair meetings, the rector was not the key office in relation to parish government: this role belonged to the two churchwardens. In many parishes churchwardens were selected yearly by the vestry to serve a one-year term, but in St Clement Danes a number of 17th-century churchwardens exceeded a year in office. By the 1690s a two-year term was the norm. Only one new warden was selected every year, with the incumbent warden taking on the mantel of the 'upper' or 'senior' warden for his remaining year in office.[11] The office was unpaid, as were all offices within the system of compulsory service that parishes in England relied on. The churchwardens had usually served in the office of overseer or collector for the poor and enjoyed a high status.

In addition to their various duties regarding the maintenance of the church and other ecclesiastical obligations, collecting church rates and keeping their accounts, the 17th-century churchwardens of St Clement Danes also undertook a range of civic administrative tasks. They led vestry committees to view parish properties to assess their state and value, inspected repairs to streets and bridges, managed annuities and were responsible for collecting rates levied for church rebuilding.[12] The junior of the two churchwardens was assigned the role of feoffee collector, which required him to collect, record, and manage revenues from the parish's charity estate in Holborn.[13] The churchwardens also controlled the parochial finances and access to the chests containing the parish cash.[14] From 1690 onwards all incoming wardens had to provide a £500 security before they could take office.[15] In the absence of the rector the vestry meeting would be chaired by one or both of the churchwardens and, as with the rector, they were ex-officio members of the vestry until the reforms of the late 19th century.

---

8   Somerville, *Savoy*, 170.
9   e.g. Hugh Mills, WCA, St CD Vestry Mins, B1060, 7 Feb. 1695.
10   *1st Annual Rpt of the Westminster City Council*, (1900), typescript available from WCA, p. 18 and p. 21; Webb, *Parish*, 36–7. Westminster was made a City in 1900.
11   e.g. Hugh Mills, WCA, St CD Vestry Mins, B1060, 7 Feb. 1695.
12   WCA, St CD Vestry Mins, B1058, 23 Sept. 1668, 20 July 1668, B1060, 5 Jan. 1686, B1058, 10 Mar. 1670.
13   WCA, St CD Vestry Mins, B1058, 18 Mar.1669, 20 Oct. 1673, B1060, 23 Dec. 1687, 7 June 1689, 2 Mar. 1693.
14   WCA, St CD Vestry Mins, B1058, 3 July 1668, 16 Oct. 1668, 9 Apr. 1669, 20 Oct. 1673.
15   WCA, St CD Vestry Mins, B1060, 21 Apr. 1690.

Figure 18 *A boundary mark, which would have been affixed to a building or pavement to show the limits of the parish. St Clement was drowned with an anchor attached to his neck, hence the parish symbol.*

The overseers of the poor were responsible for collecting the poor rate from householders and distributing it amongst the parish poor, as well as occasionally finding masters for apprentices.[16] It is not entirely clear how many overseers the parish recruited at this time, and the vestry minutes offer no indication as to the method of their selection. However, by the early 18th century there were four or five overseers and, as with other Westminster parishes, they were selected by the vestry and confirmed in office by the Middlesex JPs, who also audited the overseers' accounts.[17] It is also likely that the overseers were split into those covering the Westminster wards, and those covering the Savoy wards, since some overseers were noted as being 'of the Westminster side'.[18] Although the overseers of St Clement Danes, as elsewhere, were nominally under the control of the Middlesex JPs, it was the vestry that managed their routine business.[19] As with all compulsory parish offices, those elected for the post of overseer could choose to avoid service by paying a fine.[20]

16   Webb, *Parish*, 30–2; F. Sheppard, *Local Government in Marylebone: 1688–1835* (1958), 11, 19, 35. For finding masters see WCA, St CD Vestry Mins, B1058, 23 Apr. 1669, 14 Aug. 1673; B1060, 1 Dec. 1697.
17   WCA, St CD Vestry Mins, B1061, 30 Dec. 1700; Hatton, London, I, 207; WCA, St CD Vestry Mins, B1060, 17 Feb. 1698.
18   For example, WCA, St CD Vestry Mins, B1060, 31 Oct. 1690, 16 Apr. 1694.
19   Webb, *Parish*, 30–2; Sheppard, *Marylebone*, 35.
20   Webb, *Parish*, 18; WCA, St CD Vestry Mins, B1060, 10 Apr. 1699.

The final officer appointed primarily by the parish vestry was the vestry clerk. The first mention of a clerk was in 1668, although the term appears rarely in the vestry minutes thereafter.[21] It seems that, on some occasions, one of the churchwardens held the office alongside his wardenship, although whether this was a commonplace arrangement is unclear.[22] The 17th-century clerks entered information into the burial registers, and presumably were the author of all other parish documentation.[23]

The Westminster Court of Burgesses had responsibility for regulating trade in the parish as set out in the ordinances of 1585, appointing searchers to check the quality of butchers' produce and regulating weights and measures. A typical entry in the minutes of the court saw a butcher of Butchers' Row fined 13s. 4d. for 'two short muggs'.[24] Other trades such as brewers and particularly bakers had their produce checked for price and quality.[25] The court leet of the Duchy Liberty held similar responsibilities modelled on the Westminster ordinances, with checks carried out by aleconners (who checked the quality of produce and measures used by beer sellers) and flesh-tasters (who regulated the quality of meat and poultry sold).[26]

Circa 1700–64

The reason we are aware of the vestry's claim to select status was a major dispute in 1700 over the election of the churchwardens. This dispute led to the legal founding of a select vestry. Perversely, it also marked the beginning of a slow shift to a more democratic vestry, which culminated in a Parliamentary Act of 1764. The antecedents of the dispute lay in the vestry's willingness to embark on various costly renovations and the eventual rebuilding of the parish church. In 1668–70 a total of £2,000 was spent on contracting two masons, Joshua Marshall and Stephen Switzer, to undertake work on the church spire. [27] The vestry ordered that the money was to be raised partly from new charges for the tolling of the church bell at weddings and funerals, and partly from a general tax on the inhabitants of the parish for a period of five years.[28] In 1680 the vestry agreed a contract with masons John Shorthose and Edward Pearse to rebuild the entire church (the steeple was retained) under the supervision of Sir Christopher Wren.[29] The new church, finished in 1682, cost nearly £15,000, and left the parish nearly £4,000 in debt.[30] Even as late as 1686, the parish still owed Shorthose £1,000 for his work and was paying 5 per cent interest on the debt, an indication of the financial pressure the church rebuilding had placed upon parochial resources.[31]

---

21 WCA, St CD Vestry Mins, B1058, 23 Aug. 1668.
22 e.g. Robert Smith: WCA, St CD Vestry Mins, B1060, 17 June 1686.
23 WCA, St CD Vestry Mins, B1060, 6 Apr. 1693.
24 WCA, *Minutes of the Court of Burgesses*, WCB3, 19 June 1705.
25 W.H. Manchee, *The Westminster City Fathers 1585–1901* (1924), 212–21.
26 Somerville, *Savoy*, 156 and appendix II; J. Ritson (ed.), *A digest of the proceedings of the Court Leet and of the manor and liberty of the Savoy, parcel of the Duchy of Lancaster, in the County of Middlesex; from the year 1682 to the present time* (1789), 1–2, 30–2.
27 WCA, St CD Vestry Mins, B1058, 29 May 1668WCA, St CD Vestry Mins, B1058, 26 Mar. 1669, 20 May 1669.
28 WCA, St CD Vestry Mins, B1058, 29 June 1669, 19 Sept. 1670, 9 Nov. 1669.
29 *VCH Middx* XIII, 166.
30 Ibid., 165.
31 WCA, St CD Vestry Mins, B1060, 17 June 1686.

The burden for extricating the parish from this particularly perilous financial plight was once again placed upon the inhabitants of the parish. In 1697 the churchwardens and vestry obtained the right to levy an additional poor rate on the parishioners.[32] Receipts attached to the original indenture between the masons and the churchwardens indicate that as of October 1682, the total paid for works on the church was £3,571, well below the total cost of £15,000 claimed in 1697.[33] The interest charges on the £1,000 owed to Shorthose, and other instances of money being borrowed at interest by the parish in the 1680s, hints that some of the debt caused by rebuilding the church may well have accrued from borrowing costs. It was apparently this debt with which the vestry had saddled the parish, and their general 'mismanagement and extravagance' when it came to the parish finances, that so vexed the inhabitants and roused them to action.[34]

In 1699 a dispute occurred between the overseers and a large group of inhabitants, and the vestry over the latter's alleged financial corruption and its behaviour in electing a new churchwarden at a secret meeting.[35] The inhabitants felt they had the right to elect the churchwardens. The dispute was due to be heard and resolved by the court of the archdeacon of Middlesex. The rector of St Clement Danes, Dr George Bramston, obtained a writ of mandamus from the Court of King's Bench at Westminster, and promptly swore in the vestry's choice of churchwardens before the archdeacon's court could hear the case. In response, a number of parishioners occupied the vestry room, barred the select vestry from entering, and declared themselves to be the vestry by 'public contract'.[36] Furthermore, the two men elected as churchwardens by the parishioners obtained a writ of mandamus from the King's Bench, which ordered Bramston to swear them into office instead. The case was finally resolved by the King's Bench in favour of the parishioners.[37]

This judgement led the parishioners to set out a much more democratic and structured approach to the election of churchwardens and overseers. Electoral protocols were established, public notice of elections was to be given, and all inhabitants had the right to attend and vote. The existing senior churchwarden would nominate six men for the post who had previously held the office of overseer. The inhabitants would then select two men from this cohort as their new churchwardens. If the inhabitants present at the meeting did not approve of the six men nominated by the churchwarden, they could simply nominate and elect two men of their own choosing. The incumbent overseers were to nominate eight or more suitable inhabitants of the parish to be their successors, and the inhabitants would recommend four of the eight, or any other men they felt fit, to the JPs.[38]

Furthermore, thanks to the accusations of corruption and embezzlement of parish funds on the part of the existing vestry, there was to be a radical overhaul in terms of the transparency of the financial affairs of the parish. Thenceforth the churchwardens and overseers would transact all the business of the parish in the vestry room or

32   VCH *Middx* XIII, 165.
33   BL, Add. Ch. 1605.
34   Bodl. Rawlinson B. 377, 27 Mar. 1701, f. 3.
35   *Middx County Rec. Sess. Bks 1689–1709*, Dec. 1699, 41.
36   Bodl. Rawlinson B. 377, 27 Mar. 1701, f. 2.
37   WCA, St CD Vestry Mins, B1061, 30 Dec. 1700.
38   Ibid.

church house and deposit the parish account books there at the end of the year so that inhabitants could inspect the accounts. In addition, the overseers were ordered to have their account books audited monthly by the vestry to ensure that money collected and received for the relief of the poor was not misappropriated.[39]

This outbreak of democracy was short-lived. In March 1701 the rector of St Clement Danes, Dr Gregory Hascard, raised a petition with the Bishop of London against the parishioners for violating the rights of the ancient vestry. The petition requested that the bishop make a visitation to the parish.[40] It appears that this visitation resulted in a bishop's faculty and the establishment of a select vestry on the basis of this faculty.[41] The creation of a select vestry by bishop's faculty marks St Clement Danes out as unusual – perhaps unique – in the context of the nine civil Westminster parishes, as the use of such instruments for this purpose had virtually died out by 1700. The majority of the select vestries of Westminster were created by the Act for the Building of Fifty New Churches (1711) or individual church building acts.[42] The dispute of 1700 established the St Clement Danes vestry's select status and, as with other select vestries, the membership of the body would be replenished upon the death of a vestryman or his departure from the parish by co-option.[43] Yet throughout the 18th century the exact nature of St Clement Danes' vestry was far more complex than a simple 'open' or 'close' dichotomy.

One area where the dispute of 1700 did instigate immediate changes was in the process of the election of churchwardens. Prior to 1700 the new wardens were co-opted by the vestry.[44] After 1700, and in line with changes demanded by the militant inhabitants, the vestry adopted an elective system. Each April six men – three from the Westminster Liberty, and three from the Duchy Liberty – were nominated by the vestry, who would then select two men from the six to serve as churchwardens.[45] Spring vestry meetings developed into the fulcrum of the parish's administrative calendar, when new vestrymen were appointed, churchwardens elected, new parish offices filled and the churchwardens' and other committee accounts were audited.[46]

It is also clear that despite its select nature the vestry was unwilling, or simply unable, to debar inhabitants from all parish business. St Clement Danes was one of those metropolitan parishes such as St Mary-le-Strand, or St Leonard's, Shoreditch, where

39 WCA, St CD Vestry Mins, B1061, 30 Dec. 1700.
40 Bodl. Rawlinson B, 377. 27 Mar. 1701, f. 1.
41 Webb, *Parish*, 190–97. However, several entries in the vestry minutes make reference to the faculty – for example in relation to the creation of the office of parish clerk in 1706 (WCA, St CD Vestry Mins, B1061, 6 May 1706.), and in 1716 when, in relation to dispute over the right of the overseers to sit on the vestry, the vestry requested that 'the Faculty of the late Bishop of London for holding a Vestry' be read out (WCA, St CD Vestry Mins, B1063, 15 Nov. 1716). Maitland noted in 1739 that St Clement Danes was a faculty vestry of 44 men, W. Maitland, *The History of London from its Foundations by the Romans to the Present Time* (1739), 718.
42 Sheppard, *Marylebone*, 102; *Annual Rpt WCC*, 14.
43 E.g. the 'election' of Jeremiah Thornehill, WCA, St CD Vestry Mins, B1060, 22 Sept. 1693, and the appointment of vestrymen in 1710, WCA, St CD Vestry Mins, B1062, 13 Apr. 1710.
44 E.g. Hugh Mills, WCA, St CD Vestry Mins, B1060, 7 Feb. 1695.
45 E.g. WCA, St CD Vestry Mins, B1062, 10 Apr. 1710, and B1065, 1 Apr. 1736.
46 E.g. WCA. St CD Vestry Mins, B1063, 29 Mar. 1725; 2 Apr. 1725, 5 Apr. 1725; B1068, 16–17 Apr. 1750, 20 Apr. 1750, 1 May 1750; B1071, 17 Apr. 1775, 21 Apr. 1775, 25 Apr. 1775, 1 May 1775.

Figure 19 *St Clement Danes church in 1753, with carriages passing along the Strand.*

powers were shared between the close body and the inhabitants.[47] By the 1720s the St Clement Danes vestry was holding what were called 'general meetings', which included all inhabitants paying scot and lot. A general vestry was called for the election of churchwardens and the passing of their accounts,[48] but more often they were called when significant decisions needed to be reached on issues that affected all householders. They usually related to the parlous state of the parish finances, such as in 1723 when a general meeting was called as the parish was £3,725 in debt and had run up a further debt of £1,133 with workmen undertaking repairs to the church, presumably a reference to the raising of the church tower in 1720.[49]

Occasionally the numbers of inhabitants attending exceeded the capacity of the vestry room and they had to adjourn to the church itself.[50] Examples include in 1737 when the parish, in the grip of yet another financial crisis, required a general vestry to debate and authorise the churchwardens to draw on money from the Holborn Estate's revenues – revenues that were technically supposed to fund poor relief only – to pay its creditors.[51] Finally, general meetings were also prominent between the 1740s and 1760s when considering the issue of poor relief and the construction of a workhouse in the parish. [52]

47   Webb, *Parish*, 228.
48   E.g. WCA, St CD Vestry Mins, 14 Apr. 1735, 1 May 1735.
49   WCA, St CD Vestry Mins, B1063, 13 June 1723; VCH *Middx* XIII, 166; WCA, St CD Vestry Mins, B1063, 27 June 1723; B1063, 9 July 1723; B1063, 23 July 1723.
50   WCA, St CD Vestry Mins, B1064, 10 Apr. 1724.
51   WCA, St CD Vestry Mins, B1065, 15 Dec. 1737.
52   WCA, St CD Vestry Mins, B1066, 17 Oct. 1740, 23 Jan. 1741, 19 Feb. 1741; B1069, 6 Aug. 1759.

The select or faculty vestry continued to operate alongside the general vestry and dealt with all other business, including the nomination of churchwardens and the auditing of their accounts.[53] This binary vestry, by no means unique, remained in place until 1764 when, in contrast to the general consolidation of the close vestry system within the metropolis, the open status of the vestry of St Clement Danes was effectively enshrined in legislation.[54]

From 1764 to 1855

The vestry decided in late 1763 that the inhabitants of St Clement Danes should petition Parliament for a bill to enable the parish to construct a workhouse and manage the nightwatch and beadles. The resultant act, granted in early 1764, contained several important developments in terms of the operation of vestry government within the parish. In many ways the act codified and cemented many of the procedures that had been in operation since the early 18th century and should be seen as part of the broader evolution of vestry government in St Clement Danes.

The act stated that on or after 1 May every year, the vestry should assemble to elect up to 24 'substantial citizens' to be directors and governors of the nightwatch and beadles and to set the poor rate. Notice of these meetings was to be given in church on the Sunday before. The act also stated that on or before 29 September every year the parish account books would be audited at a vestry meeting. The books were held by the vestry clerk and he was to make them available for inspection by any of the parish inhabitants at 'all reasonable times'. Furthermore, on the Wednesday in Easter week (or within ten days thereafter) the churchwardens and vestry were to meet to appoint ten assistants to the wardens and overseers. A final clause stated that parish inhabitants were able to attend any meetings the governors, churchwardens and overseers held in relation to issues of the workhouse and the nightwatch.[55]

The vast majority of vestry business surrounded the issues covered in the act: poor relief, rates, policing and the nightwatch. Taken as a whole, these measures effectively rendered the close vestry system obsolete in St Clement Danes. It seems that after 1764, vestry meetings were genuinely 'open' affairs, although most meetings consisted of perhaps a dozen men. There was a core group of vestrymen who attended most meetings and oversaw the routine administrative business of the parish. Several important matters, notably debates held in 1770 over the erection of the parish workhouse witnessed a number of significant gatherings.[56] Large vestry meetings were also actively encouraged in some instances. At a vestry meeting on 16 January 1817, regarding the vexed issue of the cost of church repairs, 23 named vestrymen and 'many other inhabitants' were in attendance. Not only had the usual notice of the meeting been given in church on the

53   E.g. WCA, St CD Vestry Mins, B1066, 18, 19, 20, 23 Apr. 1742; B1068 16, 17, 20 Apr. 1750.

54   Sheppard, *Marylebone*, 102–21; Webb, *Parish*, 228–30.

55   PA, HL/PO/PU/1/1764/4G3n75, Public Act, 4 Geo. III, c. 55, *An Act for establishing a regular and nightly Watch, and for maintaining, regulating and employing the Poor within the Parish of Saint Clement Danes, in the Liberty of Westminster, and County of Middlesex.*

56   WCA, St CD Vestry Mins, B1071, 14 June 1770, 9 Aug. 1770, 18 Oct. 1770.

preceding Sunday, but a hand bill was also delivered to each house in the parish giving notice of the meeting.[57]

Householder voting for the election of some parish officers was another feature of the vestry. Normally the election of the parish officers was a formality, whereby the incumbent was re-elected unanimously via an apparently perfunctory show of hands in the vestry meeting. On occasion, when the incumbent was challenged or the post had become vacant, a general poll of householders could be called. The vestry minutes for the first half of the 19th century are littered with numerous instances when the vestry was adjourned to the court room due to numbers present, or when the election of a parish officer was arrived at via a householder poll.[58] These polls often lasted several days. For the election of the vestry keeper in 1820, a total of 1,135 votes were cast over a three-day period.[59] Participation by householders in the vestry – based on custom within the parish and finding its legislative voice in the 1764 act – was clearly a defining characteristic of administrative life in St Clement Danes from the early 18th century onwards. Consequently, three important early 19th-century acts – the Regulation of Parish Vestries Acts of 1818 and 1819, and the Vestries Act of 1831 – never applied to the parish.[60]

From 1855 to 1901

The Metropolis Management Act of 1855 saw St Clement Danes become part of the Strand District Board of Works (SBW), together with St Anne Soho, St Paul Covent Garden, the Savoy Precinct, St Mary-le-Strand and the Liberty of the Rolls. The vestry of St Clement Danes was obliged to elect 15 of the 49 men serving on the district board; the other constituent parishes also provided board members, ranging from one for the Savoy, to 18 for St Anne Soho, where meetings of the board were held. Each year the SBW elected one man to serve on the Metropolitan Board of Works (MBW).[61]

As part of the 1855 act, compulsory reforms to the selection and composition of the Westminster vestries including St Clement Danes were introduced, based upon the Vestries Act of 1831. The existing system of 'open' vestry government in St Clement Danes was swept away. The act stated that the size of the vestry should be based on the number of households within the parish rated at £40 or more. A parish with up to a 1,000 such households would have 18 vestrymen, 2,000 householders 24 vestrymen, and for every additional 1,000 householders thereafter an additional 12 vestrymen were added, up to a maximum of 120. St Clement Danes elected only 24 vestrymen which, as it was a populous parish, illustrates its relative poverty by the mid 19th century.[62] The voting system was effectively on a three-year cycle, with one third of the vestrymen replaced every year, which achieved an element of continuity and stability.

57   WCA, St CD Vestry Mins, B1076, 16 Jan. 1817.
58   E.g. WCA, St CD Vestry Mins, B1076, 1, 2 Oct. 1818; B1078, 6 Apr.1830, 7 Oct. 1830, 14 Oct. 1830; B1080, 10 Mar. 1854.
59   WCA, St CD Vestry Mins, B1076, 12 June 1820.
60   These acts were more commonly known as the Sturges Bourne Acts, and Hobhouse's Act respectively.
61   PA, HL/PO/PU/1/1855/18&19V1n313, Public General Act, 18 & 19 Vic. I, c. 120, *An Act for the better Local Management of the Metropolis.*
62   *Act for the better Local Management of the Metropolis*, clause II.

In order to be eligible to vote in the annual elections, a householder had to be assessed at a rateable value of £40 p.a. or more. The vote was taken by a show of hands, or, if specifically demanded by five or more householders, via a ballot. The vestry decided to hold elections in early June, to coincide with the elections for the SBW members. At least 21 days' notice had to be given prior to the vote. In addition, five auditors of the accounts were elected annually by the householders under the 1855 act. The candidates for these posts had to meet the same qualifying criteria as the candidates for vestrymen, but could not be vestrymen themselves. All issues raised at meetings were to be decided by a majority vote. Finally, the selection of the men to serve on the district boards was undertaken by the vestry at elections held on the first Wednesday of every June, using the same three-year cycle as for vestrymen. In 1856 an amendment to the act of 1855 transferred all powers over church affairs to the elected vestries.[63]

The rates of the vestry regime caused ongoing controversy within the parish, as numerous inhabitants refused to pay and the rate set was challenged in the Court of Queen's Bench.[64] Another challenge was made in the same court, alleging that the sitting vestrymen had not paid their rates and were ineligible for election. The vestrymen wanted a swift and amicable resolution, so agreed to a new election in ten days.[65] In the intervening period, the St Clement Danes representatives to the SBW stopped attending due to their legal difficulties and then resigned.[66] An election followed which pitted two lists of candidates against each other, the 'reds' of the Liberal Reform Association and the 'blues' to which the churchwardens belonged, the latter winning all 24 seats.[67] New representatives were duly elected to the SBW.[68] Parishioners continued to be charged at the petty sessions for non-payment of the rates and a stormy Easter vestry lasting nearly four hours ensued.[69] Eventually the court found it was unlawful to prevent parishioners from voting in vestry elections for non-payment.[70]

Open meetings of the ratepayers of the parish were later held in the new vestry hall, built on the site of two collapsed houses between Clement's Inn Passage and St Clement's Lane by the architects Francis Cadogan and John Butler in 1875.[71] Meetings were still held on an annual basis to set the church rate, and any ratepayer was entitled to attend.[72] The Local Government Act of 1888 abolished the by now universally derided and discredited MBW, and created in its stead the London County Council. Despite removing the MBW, the 1888 act retained the district boards – including the Strand District Board

---

63 PA, HL/PO/PU/1/1856/19&20V1n251, Public General Act, 19 & 20 Vic. I, c. 112, *An Act to amend the Act of the last Session of Parliament, Chapter One hundred and twenty, for the better Local Management of the Metropolis*. WCA, *Annual Report WCC*, 19.

64 *Daily News*, 19 Mar. 1856.

65 *Daily News*, 21 Jan. 1856.

66 WCA, SBW1, 16 Jan., 23 Jan. and 6 Feb. 1856.

67 *Daily News*, 23 Feb. 1856.

68 WCA, SBW1, 27 Feb. 1856.

69 *Daily News*, 19 Mar. 1856; *Morning Chronicle*, 26 Mar. 1856.

70 *Morning Chronicle*, 16 June 1856.

71 W.M. Stern, 'Clements Inn Passage (Clare Market) 1687–1921', *The Genealogists' Mag.*, 15:13 (1968), 488.

72 WCA, St CD Vestry Mins, B1084, 24 Feb. 1875; B1083, 11 June 1858; B1103, 27 Apr. 1894.

– as district councils.[73] The vestry of St Clement Danes continued to elect members for the Strand District Board, right up until the vestry and the board were terminated in 1900 by the London Government Act of 1899.

In 1895 the vestry minutes recorded that the vestry was elected under the Local Government Act 1894. This act abolished the rating qualification of £40 p.a.; anyone who had resided in the parish for 12 months was registered as a parochial elector and could vote. The 1894 act also removed the right of the churchwardens and incumbent to preside over meetings, and in their place a chairman was elected on a yearly basis. The last instance of the election of the 24 vestrymen and five auditors recorded in the vestry minutes was in 1893.[74] It is not entirely clear how the vestry constituted its membership in the final few years of its existence, although an entry for 7 April 1899 states that the vestry set aside the 17 May 1899 for the election of vestrymen and auditors. No details were given, but at the next meeting on 7 June 1899, the clerk was paid for acting as returning officer at the 'recent election of the vestry men'.

The London Government Act of 1899 created the 28 metropolitan boroughs which formed the County of London under the control of the LCC.[75] As a result of this act, the Strand District Board and the vestry of St Clement Danes were replaced by the Metropolitan Borough of Westminster. The borough authorities assumed the few remaining municipal obligations still in the hands of the vestry. Meanwhile the act confined the churchwardens and incumbent to ecclesiastical matters, and their centuries-old ex-officio involvement in matters of local government was ended.[76] The *1st Annual Report of the Westminster City Council* printed in November 1900 noted that the soon to be defunct vestry government of St Clement Danes consisted of 24 elected vestrymen, one incumbent, two churchwardens, 15 members of the Strand District Board, four overseers and two members of the Court of Burgesses.[77]

The Westminster Court of Burgesses itself ceased to be involved in municipal government in 1889, when its duties regarding weights and measures were taken over by the London County Council. The Court of Burgesses was abolished in 1901.[78] The constables, aleconners and flesh-tasters of the Savoy were abolished by order of the Duchy of Lancaster in 1863, but the annual court continued to meet during the 20th century, albeit in an increasingly ceremonial capacity, with a lengthy hiatus due to the Second World War.[79] The Duchy Liberty also had a separate coroner, which office was combined with the Westminster coroner in 1896 and abolished in 1930.[80]

73   PA, HL/PO/PU/1/1888/51&52V1n237, Public General Act, 51 & 52 Vic. I, c. 41, *An Act to amend the Laws relating to Local Government in England and Wales, and for other purposes connected therewith.* (4b)
74   WCA, St CD Vestry Mins, B1103, 7 July 1893.
75   The City of London was also part of the County of London, although the Corporation of London remained resolutely independent, and ceded few powers to the LCC.
76   WCA, *Annual Report WCC*, 21.
77   WCA, *Annual Report WCC*, 83.
78   Manchee, *City Fathers*, 168 and 205.
79   Somerville, *Savoy*, 195–7.
80   Ibid., 188.

Policing

In policing, St Clement Danes followed a slightly different path from the other Westminster parishes. In the late 17th and early 18th century each parish had its own set of beadles, constables and nightwatchmen who were responsible for policing, appointed and directed by the Court of Burgesses. When the watch was not deemed to be sufficient, private initiatives were not uncommon. After a spate of robberies in 1690, the inhabitants of Norfolk Street gained permission from the Middlesex Sessions to maintain a watch at their own expense, which also exempted them from paying the watch rate.[81] Where it could, the Court of Burgesses protected its jurisdiction. When the constable in Drury Lane Ward tried to replace a watchman without consulting the ward burgess, he was removed from office and the burgess reaffirmed in the sole power of appointment.[82] The court leet of the Duchy Liberty appointed four constables who could appoint a substitute, assistant or deputy; refusal of the office or failure to appear before the court to be sworn in could draw hefty fines of up to £10.[83]

The Westminster burgesses appointed a beadle for St Clement's in 1707, with instructions to oversee vagrancy, disorder, dirt and paving.[84] New watch regulations were introduced by the Court of Burgesses in 1719, the first change to its organisation since its inception in 1585. They increased the number of watchmen across Westminster with 16 assigned to St Clement Danes.[85] St Clement's contributed to the cost of other shared criminal justice systems; in 1715 the parish paid £8 towards the annual salary of £50 for the keeper of the Bridewell.[86] In the 1730s the other Westminster parishes followed the example set by St James and St Georges, who had in 1735 obtained a local act that enabled them to appoint and manage their own beadles, nightwatch and set a rate. St Clement Danes was the singular exception.

Every October the individual ward burgesses nominated several householders within their wards for the posts of Westminster beadles, constables and nightwatchmen[87] The court then selected the requisite number of men from the lists to serve in these posts: in St Clement Danes, two beadles, eight constables and 28 watchmen.[88] Service in the office of constable or nightwatchman was a householder's obligation and was therefore unpaid and, in many cases, unwelcome. The vestry did start directing the beadles in the 1750s, and there was also an aborted attempt to obtain a watch act in 1750.[89] The ability to pay for a substitute meant that the watch gradually professionalised by default and the vestry

81   *LL*, Middx Sess.: Sess. papers – justices' working docs, 17 Dec. 1690, ref. LMSMPS500070018 (accessed 6 June 2017).
82   WCA, *Minutes of the Court of Burgesses*, WCB5, 25 July 1717.
83   Ritson, *A Digest*, 4–10.
84   WCA, *Minutes of the Court of Burgesses*, WCB3, 17 July 1707.
85   Manchee, *City Fathers*, 33.
86   *LL*, Westminster Sess.: Sess. papers – justices' working docs, Apr. 1715, LMWJPS653400014 (accessed 6 June 2017).
87   E. Reynolds, *Before the Bobbies: The Nightwatch and Police Reform in Metropolitan London, 1720–1830* (1998), 10.
88   Hatton, *London*, I, 206; Maitland, *London*, 718.
89   WCA, St CD Vestry Mins, B1067, 5 Jan. 1749; B1068, 15 Jan. 1750.

also became increasingly involved in its direction.[90] During the latter part of the 18th century, supplementary detective work was supplied by the Bow Street Runners based at the nearby Public Office, who drew some of their number from St Clement's, such as Patrick Macmanus of Stanhope Street.[91]

The 1764 Watch Act empowered the vestry to meet every May to appoint 24 citizens to act as directors or governors of the nightwatch and beadles. They were able to appoint as many of these men as they felt the parish required. Furthermore, they were to place in writing the duties of these officers (including the frequency of their rounds, what they could carry as arms, and their wages) and were empowered to repair the watch house. Although not stipulated in the act, the vestry decided to appoint the governors by parochial ward. The constables on duty – one from the Liberty of Westminster and one from the Duchy of Lancaster – were to keep watch and ward from 9 p.m. to 7 a.m. from 29 September to 13 March, then 10 p.m. to 5 a.m. the rest of year. Anyone they arrested or apprehended was to be taken to the JPs. Constables were also ordered to visit the watchhouses twice a night to ensure that the watchmen were fulfilling their duties and to report any miscreants to the vestry.

In order to fund the watch, the vestry was empowered to levy a yearly rate not exceeding 4d. in the pound. The rate had to be authorised by the Middlesex JPs, and would be collected quarterly by collectors appointed by the vestry. The collector's books were to be audited by the vestry once a year in late September. The first rate was set at the maximum of 4d. in the pound.[92] The watchhouse was located in the new/upper church yard and was pulled down and rebuilt as part of the construction of the workhouse in the early 1770s. As with the workhouse, the construction of this new brick built watchhouse was not without financial difficulty, and required the parish to borrow money to complete the project.[93]

Two additional acts in 1774 and 1809 offered some slight alterations to the administration and financing of the nightwatch. The first of these acts empowered the vestry to appoint a committee of five to ten men to supervise the watch and enabled the vestry to raise the rate to 6d. in the pound. It also gave the vestry power over the watch in the Duchy Liberty. The 1809 amending act allowed the parish to increase the rate to a maximum of 1s. in the pound.[94] According to the vestry, the previous maximum of 4d. in the pound had for some years been insufficient to cover the cost of the watch, and so they had taken to setting the rate – effectively illegally – at between 5d. and 6d. in the pound.[95] On occasion, extraordinary efforts were made to reduce petty crime and disorderliness. The vestry responded to the Royal Proclamation of 1787 by summoning

90   Manchee, *City Fathers*, 33.

91   J.M. Beattie, *The First English Detectives: The Bow Street Runners and the policing of London, 1750–1840* (Oxford, 2012), 60.

92   WCA, St CD Vestry Mins, B1070, 30 Aug. 1764.

93   WCA, St CD Vestry Mins, B1071, 7 Nov. 1771, 12 Nov. 1771.

94   PA, HL/PO/PB/1/1774/14G3n196, Public Act, 14 Geo. III, c. 90. *An Act for the better Regulation of the Nightly Watch and Beadles within the City and Liberty of Westminster, and Parts adjacent; and for other Purposes therein mentioned*; PA, HL/PO/PB/1/1809/49G3n248, Local Act, 49 Geo. III, c.113, *An Act for enlarging the Powers of Two Acts of His present Majesty, so far as relates to the establishing a nightly Watch, and for maintaining the Poor within the Parish of Saint Clement Danes, in the County of Middlesex.*

95   WCA, St CD Vestry Mins, B1075, 1 Aug. 1808.

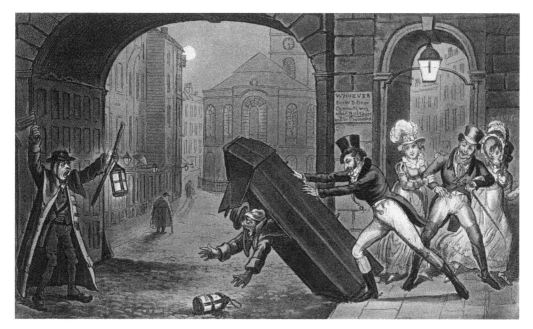

Figure 20 *An illustration to Pierce Egan's* Life in London, *showing an attack on a watchman. The scene looks westward through Temple Bar with St Clement Danes in the distance.*

their local JPs and launching a campaign against drunkenness, gaming, brothels, vagrancy and Sunday trading. They set up mechanisms by which members of the public could offer up information and threatened innkeepers that allowed such behaviour with the loss of their licence, advertising their efforts in the London newspapers.[96]

The existence of the paid and parochially managed nightwatch for St Clement Danes was relatively short lived thanks to the creation of the Metropolitan Police in 1829, which placed responsibility for policing for large parts of the capital, including Westminster, in the hands of the home secretary. The watch rate was abolished and instead, its commissioners were authorised to direct the overseers to collect a special rate for the purpose. This rate – the level of which was dictated by the commissioners, but was not to exceed 8*d*. in the pound – was collected alongside the poor rate.[97] The St Clement Danes vestry minutes only record the collection of the poor rate, suggesting that the vestry simply incorporated the collection of the police rate into that of the poor rate. The overseers were also required to pay a lump sum of £1,149 out of the poor rate in 1829, when the first warrants from the commissioners were issued.[98] By the time of its cessation in the 1820s, the old watching system within the parish consisted of 32 nightwatchmen along with four beadles.[99] One curiosity that stands out is that the parish was home to the last set of stocks in London, situated in Portugal Street and eventually removed in 1826.[100]

96   *World and Fashionable Advertiser*, 22 Aug. 1787.
97   Reynolds, *Bobbies*, 155.
98   WCA, St CD Vestry Mins, B1077, 1 Oct. 1829.
99   Ibid.
100 *Jackson's Oxford Jnl*, 12 Aug. 1826.

The vestry was not convinced as to the potential efficacy and value of the Metropolitan Police, and resolved to collude with St Leonards Shoreditch to recruit the other Westminster parishes in an unsuccessful attempt to petition Parliament to repeal the Metropolitan Police Act.[101] The collection of the rate by the overseers to fund the Metropolitan Police was the only major duty the parish had in relation to policing post-1829. Although they no longer had responsibilities in relation to policing, the parish continued to appoint two beadles until 1900. This was a largely ceremonial role, with post holders paid a small salary of £30 p.a. from the church rates.[102]

Highways and Street Cleaning

In the late 16th and 17th century, it was notionally the Burgesses that were responsible for ensuring that individual householders fulfilled their obligation to pave, cleanse and light the street in front of their abodes. The burgess for the ward was entitled to direct a small force of street cleaners known as scavengers and appointed by the Court of Burgesses from a list of householders. It is clear from the vestry minutes that by the early 18th century, the vestry was electing and managing at least two scavengers – those for the Westminster Liberty side of the parish – and having them confirmed in office by the JPs.[103] Furthermore, the vestry was levying a scavengers' rate, which mainly paid for the services of rakers at a cost of £535 p.a. by 1739, to remove the dirt and rubbish collected by the scavengers, as allowed by an act of 1690/1.[104] The issue of the scavengers' rate was one of the few that seemed to generate conflict between the vestry and the officers of the Duchy Liberty.[105] In the early 18th century the parish of St Clement Danes possessed eight scavengers. By the 1730s this had grown to sixteen men – two for each ward of the parish – who were all being elected by the vestry. The court leet of the Duchy of the Savoy amerced numerous people for encroaching on the highways (or nuisances), either with rubbish, carts or buildings.[106] It also took responsibility for many of the riverfront features of the parish, including Essex and Surrey Stairs where boats could land.[107]

The other offices related to street maintenance were the surveyors of the highways. The surveyors were responsible for ensuring the repair and maintenance of paving of the streets and the policing and clearance of obstructions from these highways. They could raise a rate when specific highway improvements were required. St Clement Danes may have been operating a system of highway surveyors supported by a rate since the 1580s.[108] Vestry minutes in 1687 record two surveyors for St Clement Danes, one for the

---

101 WCA, St CD Vestry Mins, B1078, 7 Oct. 1830, 14 Oct. 1830.
102 WCA, St CD Vestry Mins, B1078, 1 May 1830, 6 May 1830.
103 WCA, St CD Vestry Mins, B1061, 14 Mar. 1702, 5 Aug. 1707.
104 PA, HL/PO/PU/1/1690/2&3W&Mn14 Public Act, 2 William & Mary session 2, c. 8. *An Act for paving and cleaning the Streets in the Cities of London and Westminster, and Suburbs and Liberties thereof, and Out Parishes in the County of Middlesex, and in the Borough of Southwark, and other Places within the Weekly Bills of Mortality, in the County of Surrey, and for regulating the Markets therein mentioned*; Maitland, *London*, 718.
105 WCA, St CD Vestry Mins, B1064, 21 Apr. 1730.
106 Ritson, *A Digest*, 16–8 and 20–5.
107 Ibid., 14 and 28–9.
108 Somerville, *Savoy*, 191.

Westminster Liberty and the other for the Duchy Liberty.[109] In 1708 there were four such posts, and by the time of the last election in 1772, five surveyors were appointed for the Westminster side of the parish and five for the duchy side.[110]

By the late 17th and early 18th century, control over the scavengers and responsibility for street cleaning and repair had become part of the broader battle for power between the Burgesses on the one hand and the JPs and Westminster vestries on the other. In 1728 legislation allowed the Westminster JPs and vestries to appoint and oversee additional officers called 'surveyors of the street', who reported directly to the JPs when householders failed in their duty to maintain the streets.[111] An account from 1732 notes that St Clement Danes had two surveyors of the street.[112]

St Clement Danes and its sister parishes successfully opposed several bills and initiatives to reform street cleaning and maintenance within Westminster during the 1750s.[113] Institutional change was achieved when the Annoyance Jury of the Court of Burgesses was made permanent by Act of Parliament in 1756, with St Clement Danes providing a single juror of the 45 appointed. Its role was to report defective pavements and obstructions in the street. The jury also took on enforcement of the regulations respecting weights and measures, a responsibility it retained until it was taken over by a professional inspector in 1861.[114] Despite ongoing opposition from the vestry, a Westminster Paving Act was passed in 1762.[115] This created a supra-parochial body of Westminster paving commissioners, comprised of elected members from each of the Westminster parishes who oversaw street maintenance, cleaning and lighting, and were allowed to levy a rate for doing so.

The commission's cost and efficacy were repeatedly questioned by the vestry during the 1760s. In 1765 the commissioners informed the vestry that there were several streets within St Clement Danes that the commission did not cover, and the parish itself would have to take responsibility for cleaning, probably in consequence of a 1765 amendment allowing entire streets to effectively pay the commissioners to carry out repaving.[116] The vestry was apparently required to levy an additional rate and contract a raker to ensure the cleaning of these streets was undertaken.[117] The court leet of the Duchy Liberty amerced a scavenger of the commission in 1766 for not cleaning the Strand, and the commissioners of sewers in 1770.[118] The clearly unpopular paving commission was progressively sidelined by St Clement Danes and the other Westminster parishes

109 WCA, St CD Vestry Mins, B1060, 15 Apr. 1687.

110 Hatton, *London*, I, 206; Anon., *New Remarks of London* (1732), 256; WCA, St CD Vestry Mins, B1071, 18 Nov. 1772.

111 PA, HL/PO/PU/1/1728/2G2n23, Public Act, 2 Geo. II, c. 11, *An Act for better paving and cleansing the Streets in the City and Liberty of Westminster, and other Places within the Limits of the Weekly Bills of Mortality, in the County of Middlesex*.

112 Anon., *New Remarks*, 256.

113 WCA, St CD Vestry Mins, B1068, 26 Mar. 1753; B1069, 2 May 1757.

114 Manchee, *City Fathers*, 145–6.

115 WCA, St CD Vestry Mins, B1070, 3 May 1762. PA, HL/PO/PU/1/1762/2G3n104 Public Act, 2 Geo. III., c.21. *An Act for Paving, Cleansing and Lighting the Squares, Streets and Lanes within the City and Liberty of Westminster*

116 B. Webb, and S. Webb, *English Local Government: Statutory Authorities for Special Purposes* (1908) 282–3.

117 WCA, St CD Vestry Mins, B1070, 11 July 1765, 31 July 1765, 7 Aug. 1765.

118 Ritson, *A Digest*, 3–4 and 27.

over the ensuing decade. It seems that a 1769–70 Parliamentary bill instigated by the commissioners to raise the paving rate to 1s. 6d. in the pound was the catalyst for nine of the Westminster parishes obtaining an amending act in 1771 to the Westminster Paving Act.[119]

This amending act allowed each parish to elect annually between seven and 21 householders to comprise a parochial paving committee. The first meeting of the St Clement Danes committee occurred in April 1771.[120] These committees were handed rate raising and expenditure powers, and effectively usurped the paving commission. The creation of this committee also apparently ended the yearly election of the surveyors of the highways in St Clement Danes. In 1782 St George Hanover Square brought a bill before Parliament which was designed to remove the parish from the auspices of the paving commission. The St Clement Danes vestry was concerned that the removal of the parish of St George – 'the most opulent in Westminster' – from the commission would result in the remaining parishes having to increase their contribution.[121]

After an initial attempt to oppose St George Hanover Square's bill, St Clement Danes instead decided to follow suit (probably after corresponding with, and working alongside, other Westminster parishes) and petitioned Parliament for a similar bill.[122] This process resulted in the Local Act of 1783 which withdrew St Clement Danes from the jurisdiction of the paving commissioners and removed all authority to cleanse and pave the streets from the court leet of the Duchy of Lancaster, which had already lost interest in these functions.[123] The act left the committee structure established in 1771 intact, but also created a board of trustees comprised of 16 vestrymen. This first board included such local luminaries as Charles Howard, 11th duke of Norfolk (at that time styled the earl of Surrey).[124] The first committee election under this act was held in July 1783 with elections held every February thereafter.[125]

This system of street maintenance and cleaning remained largely unaltered until 1855, when the Metropolis Management Act abolished all paving committees and commissions. The act established the Metropolitan Board of Works, under which the Strand District Board was created to oversee drainage and sewerage (previously under the jurisdiction of the non-parochial Westminster Court of Sewers),[126] paving, lighting and street cleaning within its constituent parishes.[127] After 1855 the vestry was relegated to occasionally undertaking minor works at the behest of the MBW or petitioning the Board over various projects. The one area where the parish did remain directly involved

---

119 WCA, St CD Vestry Mins, B1071, 27 Mar. 1769, 5 Dec. 1770. PA, HL/PO/PU/1/1771/11G3n60. Public Act, 11 Geo. III, c. 22 *An Act to amend and render more effectual several Acts made relating to paving, cleansing and lighting the Squares, Streets, Lanes and other Places within the City and Liberty of Westminster and Parts adjacent.*

120 WCA, St CD Vestry Mins, B1071, 13 Apr. 1771.

121 WCA, St CD Vestry Mins, B1072, 30 Apr. 1782.

122 WCA, St CD Vestry Mins, B1072, 3 Feb. 1783, 17 Mar. 1783, 27 Mar. 1783, 21 Apr. 1783.

123 PA, HL/PO/PU/1/1783/23G3n100. Local Act, 23, Geo III., c.89. *An Act for better paving, cleansing and lighting the Parish of Saint Clement Danes, in the County of Middlesex, and certain Places adjoining thereto; and for removing and preventing Nuisances and Annoyances therein*; Somerville, *Savoy*, 187.

124 WCA, St CD Vestry Mins, B1072, 21 Apr. 1783.

125 WCA, St CD Vestry Mins, B1072, 1 July 1783.

126 Webb, *Parish*, 68–84.

127 *An Act for the Better Local Management of the Metropolis* (1855) clause XC.

Figure 21 Charles Howard, 11th duke of Norfolk, was a trustee responsible for paving in the parish. He was more widely known for his drinking and dislike of personal hygiene, and is depicted in discussion with a prostitute.

in the issue of paving, street maintenance and cleaning was via the overseers, who were expected to levy the sewers rate, the lighting rate and the general rate that funded the activities of the boards.[128]

128 *An Act for the Better Local Management of the Metropolis* (1855) clause CLVIII–CLXI.

Poor Relief

Poor relief provision in the parish of St Clement Danes divides into three distinct phases. The first covers the period up to 1764 and the Local Act previously described, the second through to the mid 1830s and creation of the Strand Poor Law Union, and the third until the abolition of vestry government in 1900.

Although evidence is patchy, a poor rate was certainly levied in the late 17th century, when the rate was increased as the overseers were out of money.[129] The yearly setting of the rate – if indeed the rate was set on a yearly basis – is not recorded in the minutes.[130] In the earlier part of the 18th century it was set each June. In the 17th and early 18th century the vestry minutes record lists of those in receipt of pensions and poor relief, although such information seems to disappear from the minutes by the 1720s. The parish carried out a census of its dependent poor in 1745, categorised by groups in receipt of monthly or more sporadic relief. Hitchcock and Shoemaker have analysed the 461 paupers listed and shown that older women were the largest group receiving poor relief. The average period for which paupers had been receiving relief before 1745 was 16 years.[131] The Middlesex Sessions dealt with appeals relating to poor relief in the parish and removals of poor people to their parish of residence, as well as issues relating to apprentices.[132] For cases where the overseers paid out money for poor people who were not resident in the parish, as they did for the lying in of Mary Alloway, a vagrant who gave birth to a bastard child in the parish in 1750, they could apply to the Middlesex Sessions for recompense.[133]

The vestry minutes offer little in terms of detail on the daily activities of the overseers. Their presence in the minutes increases noticeably throughout the first half of the 18th century, which along with the monthly auditing of their accounts introduced by the 1740s, undoubtedly reflects the vestry's growing concern about poor relief provision, particularly in terms of funding. Between 1730 and 1750 the cost of relief doubled, despite a declining population.[134] By the 1750s the vestry was setting the rate on a quarterly basis, presumably in order to increase flexibility when it came to raising cash to fund relief. By this time, the rate was almost certainly assessed and collected on a ward-by-ward basis by the overseers. The level of the poor rate did fluctuate throughout the late 18th and 19th century, but apparently did not exceed a level of 10*d*. in the pound.

An episode in 1754 concerning poor relief illustrates how the select and general vestries operated alongside each other, and shows Westminster parochial democracy in action. In February 1754 a vestry meeting, consisting of the churchwardens, overseers, 25 vestrymen, and 'several' other inhabitants, ordered that the faculty vestry (the select

---

129 WCA, St CD Vestry Mins, B1060, 3 July 1694.

130 WCA, St CD Vestry Mins, B1062, 11 July 1710.

131 T. Hitchcock and R. Shoemaker, *London Lives: Poverty, crime, and the making of a modern city, 1690–1800* (Cambridge, 2015), 141–2.

132 *LL*, Middx Sess.: Sess. papers – justices' working docs, e.g. 18 Apr. 1694, ref. LMSMPS500330067; July 1697, LMSMPS500500016 and 20 Dec. 1705, LMSMPS501040016 (accessed 6 June 2017).

133 *LL*, Middx Sess.: Sess. papers – justices' working docs, 10 Sept. 1750, LMSMPS504040002 (accessed 6 June 2017)

134 Hitchcock and Shoemaker, *London Lives*, 147.

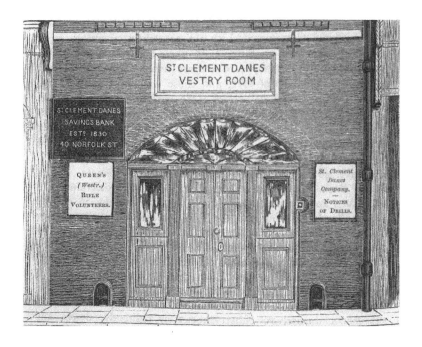

Figure 22 *The old vestry room (above), sold to the government and built over by the Royal Courts of Justice, and the new vestry hall (left) built in 1875.*

vestry) along with 11 other men form a committee to consider methods for the more effectual relief of the poor. The general vestry considered the committee's proposal to farm poor relief to a Mr Tull, at a cost of £1,668 a year. The decision as to whether to accept Tull's proposal was left to a public vote. The parish beadles were ordered to print and distribute 2,000 copies of a report on the issue to the inhabitants of the parish, and a poll was taken which lasted over two days.[135]

The 1764 Local Act empowered the churchwardens, the overseers, and ten annually elected vestrymen to act as a committee to oversee poor relief, to set the poor rate and to manage the workhouse. The committee was effectively answerable to the vestry assembled. The first rate was set at 6*d.* in the pound.[136] The committee continued to be elected on an annual basis and set the poor rate until the abolition of the vestry in 1900. A public meeting was to be held in the vestry room to agree contracts for the 'lodging, keeping, maintaining, or employing' of the poor and the construction of the workhouse. The act also stipulated that only one rate for poor relief was allowed, that landlords could be responsible for payment of the rate and confirmed that the money should be collected and accounted for on a ward-by-ward basis. Individual petitions against the rate and sanctions against non-payment were dealt with by the vestry until 1764, when appeals were redirected to the Middlesex JPs.

Clement Danes was known as the 'best "casualty parish" in London' during the 18th century, drawing poor people from other parishes to benefit from its relatively generous provision of relief.[137] Its geographical position in London caused further problems; in 1774 the constables of St Clement Danes complained that vagrants moved on from the City of London were being ejected across the border into their parish.[138] The parish also struggled with the Inns of Court and Chancery within and adjacent to it, having accrued debts of over £300 by 1776 defending actions brought for recovery of poor rates against Lincoln's Inn, Clement's Inn, Lyon's Inn and New Inn.[139] In 1779 the vestry decided to farm the rate collection to a collector who answered to the overseers. The collector was paid 2*d.* in the pound 'for so much Money as shall be Collected on the Poors Rates'.[140] In 1809, an amending act to the Local Act of 1764 gave the parish the right to appoint two or more such collectors.[141]

By the 1780s many poor children of the parish over the age of six were apprenticed to institutions outside the capital, such as silk mills in Watford.[142] In the late 18th and early 19th century, St Clement's sent particularly large numbers of apprentices into the cotton

135 WCA, St CD Vestry Mins, B1068, 21 Feb. 1754, 19 Mar. 1754, 22 May 1754, 18 June 1754.
136 WCA, St CD Vestry Mins, B1070, 9 May 1764.
137 T. Hitchcock, *Down and Out in Eighteenth-Century London* (2004), 142.
138 *LL*, Middx Sess.: Sess. papers – justices' working docs, Oct. 1774, LMSMPS506450203 (accessed 6 June 2017).
139 House of Commons, *Report from the committee appointed to make enquiries relating to the employment, relief, and maintenance, of the poor; the apprehending and passing of vagrants; and regulating houses of correction* (1776), 20.
140 WCA, St CD Vestry Mins, B1072, 10 May 1779, 21 May 1779.
141 WCA, St CD Vestry Mins, B1075, 1 Aug. 1808, 8 Sept. 1808, 22 June 1809; PA, HL/PO/PB/1/1809/49G3n248, Public Act, 49 Geo. III, c.113, *An Act for enlarging the Powers of Two Acts of His present Majesty, so far as relates to the establishing a nightly Watch, and for maintaining the Poor within the Parish of Saint Clement Danes, in the County of Middlesex.*
142 WCA, St CD Vestry Mins, B1072, 12 June 1782.

industry. The apprentices from St Clement's had one of the lowest average ages at binding of the London parishes.[143] This meant sending children far from home, with 46.3 per cent of apprentices sent long distances, mostly to the fast-growing cotton manufacturing regions of Lancashire and Glasgow. The parish had a particularly strong relationship with several industrialists, including John Birch.[144] There were also significant numbers of boys apprenticed as chimney sweepers and girls as milliners, illustrating a gender divide in the occupations assigned.[145] St Clement's was highly negligent towards its apprentices and the practice of sending apprentices far from their place of residence was outlawed in 1816.[146]

Until 1836 and the creation of the Strand Poor Law Union – initially covering the parishes of St Clement Danes, St Mary-le-Strand, St Paul Covent Garden, the Duchy of Lancaster, the Savoy Precinct, and the Liberty of the Rolls – poor relief in St Clement Danes was paid for by a poor rate, levied by the vestry assembled, collected by the overseers, and distributed by the overseers with occasional interventions by the vestry. It was the JPs who confirmed overseers in office, sanctioned the yearly poor rate, signed off the overseers' accounts and adjudicated in any disputes over the collection or disbursement of the poor rate, but it was only in relation to the last of these duties that the JPs infrequently appear in the vestry minutes.

The remit of the overseers was much altered by the transferral of power over poor relief from the vestry in 1836, but they were still responsible at a parochial level for the collection of the rates. A number of offices that had emerged over the years to assist the overseers in administration of poor relief – including the clerk to the overseers, the assistant clerk, and the messenger – were abolished as a consequence of the 1836 reforms.[147] Perhaps unsurprisingly, the issue of setting the poor rate engendered considerable interest within the vestry: debates and disputes over the level of the rate appear in the vestry minutes across the period. Invariably, disagreement arose when the vestry assembled felt that the rate proposed by the poor relief committee was too high. When disputes did occur, such as in October 1850, the setting of the rate was left to an open vote within the vestry.[148]

The Workhouse

The vestry minutes in 1673 make reference to a workhouse in Lincoln's Inn. Several other references scattered throughout the late 17th and early 18th-century minutes suggest that the workhouse during this period may have had a daily workshop located in the new church yard (also known as the upper church yard), run by a series of contractors, where

143 A. Levene, 'Parish apprenticeship and the old poor law in London', *Econ. Hist. Rev*, 63:4 (2010), 926, 932.

144 Levene, 'Parish apprenticeship', 936; K. Honeyman, *Child Workers in England, 1780–1820: Parish apprentices and the making of the early industrial labour force* (Farnham, 2007), 27, 40, 59–60.

145 K.D.M. Snell, *Annals of the Labouring Poor: Social change and agrarian England, 1660–1900,* (Cambridge, 1985), 287–9.

146 Honeyman, *Child Workers in England*, 221.

147 WCA, St CD Vestry Mins, B1079, 6 Oct. 1836.

148 WCA, St CD Vestry Mins, B1080 24 Oct. 1850.

Figure 23 *In Holles Street, Clare Market, a woman with a baby stands near a sign offering 'lodgings for women'. In the background a woman is stood near a well-dressed man, possibly begging.*

the poor were engaged in activities such as spinning.[149] In 1708 the parish, along with St Martin-in-the-Fields, was involved in an abortive attempt to secure an Act of Parliament to establish a permanent workhouse.[150] The vestry took the decision in 1727 to demolish the watch house and almshouses (along with an inn) on the upper church yard site, and build a workhouse for 200 hundred people at a total cost of £1,700.[151] This initiative floundered in the face of opposition to the cost; an increase in the rate would have been required to fund the construction. Many further efforts to prompt the construction of a workhouse throughout the 1730s, '40s and '50s suffered similar fates.[152]

The 1764 act empowered a committee to manage the workhouse, but the difficulty of raising the capital required to fund construction remained.[153] The vestry had to resort to a further Act of Parliament, based on previous such acts obtained by the parishes of Whitechapel, Aldgate, Shoreditch, Greenwich and others, that allowed the vestry to sell annuities set against the poor rate to fund the project.[154] The parish ran a set of almshouses in the upper or new church yard in Portugal Street, the earliest reference to

149 Mention of a workhouse in Lincoln's Inn in WCA, St CD Vestry Mins, B1058, 16 Oct. 1673, and further mentions of a workhouse in B1060, 7 June 1689; B1061 (undated) Mar. 1705, 26 June 1705, 23 Oct. 1707.
150 WCA, St CD Vestry Mins, B1061, 17 Dec. 1708.
151 WCA, St CD Vestry Mins, B1064, 17 May 1727.
152 Hitchcock and Shoemaker, *London Lives*, 297.
153 WCA, St CD Vestry Mins, B1070, 9 May 1764.
154 E.g. for Greenwich see 26 Geo. 2 c.100; WCA, St CD Vestry Mins, B1071, 4 Dec. 1767, 28 Dec. 1770.

which was in 1693.[155] The Portugal Street building apparently measured 86 ft by 17 ft.[156] The 12 poor women in each house received 2s. per week. One contemporary account notes that the upper churchyard consisted of six almshouses with six rooms, although they were removed to make room for the new workhouse.[157]

In the meantime, the reformer Jonas Hanway was releasing statistics about the high death rate of infants in the parish, particularly at a nursing home run for the parish by Hannah Poole.[158] St Clement Danes' treatment of children and apprentices was brought under a new regulatory framework by an Act of Parliament promoted by Hanway in 1768, which brought the parish into line with more widespread practice, but its problem with high infant mortality rates continued.[159] Financial obstacles ensured that it was not until 1771 that construction on the workhouse building actually began.[160] Further sales of annuities were required to ensure that the project was completed in 1773.[161] The buildings were of brick and housed 30 apartments as well as offices.[162] During its construction the parish insured the workhouse for the value of £4,000, giving some indication as to its construction costs and the significant investment that this building represented for the parish.[163]

Concern over the cost of the workhouse was a recurring theme. In 1781 the churchwardens and overseers proposed that the parish farm out the management of the workhouse to a contractor, thereby saving the parish an estimated £800 a year, although the proposal was rejected.[164] A master of the workhouse, alongside other salaried officers such as the matron, the surgeon and the apothecary, were elected by the vestry annually.

The overseers, churchwardens and their assistants continued to introduce orders and resolutions to improve the management of the workhouse which were then confirmed at a public vestry meeting. Orders passed in 1785 included asking the master of the workhouse to record the name and age of every new inmate and if they were discharged or had died, so that he could present it monthly to the board of assistants and they could inspect inmates regarding their settlement and fitness to work.[165] After the death of the workhouse master, Benjamin Wingrove, in 1791, expenses at the workhouse began to spiral out of control so that in 1797 the vestry set up a committee to investigate.[166] They

---

155 WCA, St CD Vestry Mins, B1060, 2 Nov. 1693.

156 WCA, St CD Vestry Mins, B1066, 23 Oct. 1740.

157 Anon, *New Remarks*, 256

158 J. Hanway, *Letters on the importance of the rising generation of the laboring part of our fellow-subjects; being an account of the miserable state of the infant parish poor* (1967), 25–6; Hitchcock and Shoemaker, *London Lives*, 291.

159 Hitchcock and Shoemaker, *London Lives*, 295; A. Levene, *The Childhood of the Poor: Welfare in Eighteenth Century London* (Houndmills, 2012), 56.

160 WCA, St CD Vestry Mins, B1071, 24 Jan. 1771.

161 Ibid., 25 Mar. 1772.

162 House of Commons, *Report from the committee appointed to make enquiries relating to the employment, relief, and maintenance, of the poor; the apprehending and passing of vagrants; and regulating houses of correction* (1776), 19.

163 WCA, St CD Vestry Mins, B1071, 5 Sept. 1771.

164 WCA, St CD Vestry Mins, B1072, 5 Apr. 1781.

165 WCA, St CD Vestry Mins, B1072, 7 Apr. 1785; 'An Alphabetical List of Persons in the House 7 Feb 1785', B1247.

166 WCA, St CD Vestry Mins, B1074, 17 Apr. 1791; St CD Vestry Mins, B1074, 2 Nov. 1797

found a vast increase in consumables from candles to food and beer, such that among other economies, brewing in the workhouse was discontinued. The posts of master and matron of the workhouse were to be elected annually, when they would present printed accounts.[167]

In 1836 the Strand Poor Law Union was formed which built a Union workhouse in Cleveland Street. As a result, the St Clement Danes workhouse in Portugal Street was closed. The building was subsequently occupied from 1840 onwards by King's College Hospital. The parish eventually sold the freehold of the land to the hospital for a perpetual rental charge of £240 p.a.[168] The hospital remained in the parish until moving to Denmark Hill, near Camberwell (Surr.) where building of new premises began in 1909.[169]

St Clement Danes Parochial Charities

Poor relief in St Clement Danes also relied heavily on charity, which lay outside the remit of the vestry, although the overlapping interests and large sums of money involved meant that charitable donations easily became entangled in vestry politics. There were numerous charitable donations made to ameliorate different aspects of the lives of poor residents of St Clement Danes. Between 1480 and 1660, parishioners in St Clement Danes provided £4463 13s. to charity.[170] As well as those charities described below which were specific to St Clement Danes, there were also a large number of charities that were established in other Westminster parishes and either from commencement, or at a later date, extended their scope to include St Clement Danes. These charities are outside the scope of this work, but include the Thomas Arneway Charity which provided loans to individuals, Earl Craven's Pest House Charity and the Westminster Amalgamated Charity.

Of the parochial bequests made before 1660, the oldest was Robert Read's, who gave 20s. p.a. in 1568 for the poor of St Clement Danes. A large early bequest of £200 was left by Robert Cecil, earl of Salisbury in his will of 1612 for the poor of St Martin-in-the-Fields and St Clement Danes, which still regularly paid out in the 19th century.[171] Other charities provided coals, interest-free loans, disbursements to poor widows, payment for a sermon from a poor minister, and money for the education of poor boys and girls, chimney sweeps and residents of the parish almshouses.[172] The charities drew income from investments, rent-charges and properties, both within and beyond the parish boundaries. Properties in the parish that paid out to local charities were knocked down as part of redevelopments at various times triggering lump sum payments. These included two houses on the north side of St Clement's churchyard which were sold in 1793 to the City of London under legislation for improving the approaches to Temple

167 WCA, St CD Vestry Mins, B1074, 5 Apr. 1798.
168 WCA, St CD Vestry Mins, B1080, 7 Feb. 1850, 10 May 1850.
169 Hearnshaw, *King's College London 1828–1928*, 420.
170 W.K. Jordan *The Charities of London 1480–1660* (1960), 41–2
171 *Endowed Charities London,* V (1903), 25–6 & 62; WCA B1076, 266
172 *Endowed Chars London,* V, 23–5, 27–8, 62–4 & 79; WCA 2081/2; B1076, 264–8; B1299; B1300, 296 and 324; B1309; B1320.

Bar, a house on Butchers' Row and another on Holywell Street, both sold under the 1806 Temple Bar Improvement Act to the City of London.[173]

The St Clement Danes Parochial Charities brought the following charities and their endowments together under an Order of the Charity Commissioners in 1880: Robert Read, John Vale, William Bissell, Harman Warner, Edward Price, Nicholas Backhouse, Margaret Forster, Robert, earl of Salisbury, Mudford (first name unknown), Richard Jacob, Richard Beddoe, Hester Wright, Richard Twining, Rupertia Hill, Lady Middleton, Lady Bridgeman, William Lawrence, Richard Shalmer, John Shaw, Ann Webb and the properties in Butchers' Row and Holywell Street. The income of the charity was applied as follows: to the rector of St Clement Danes 40s. for preaching a sermon in the parish church on New Year's Day; 20s. for a sermon on 25 March; 20s. for a sermon on Good Friday; 42s. for sermons on Good Friday and Christmas Day; 10s. 6d. to the curate for reading prayers on Good Friday and Christmas Day; and 42s. to churchwardens towards lighting the church on Good Friday and Christmas Day and general purposes of the church.

From these same charities £100 (£50 from 1888) was paid for the benefit of deserving residents in the parish, through one or more of the following: (a) Subscriptions or donations to dispensary, infirmary or hospital to secure benefits for the objects of the charities. (b) Subscriptions or donations to any provident club or society for supply of coal, clothing or other necessaries. (c) Subscriptions or donations in aid of provident or friendly association acceptable to the inhabitants of St Clement Danes. (d) Contributions towards cost of outfit on entering a trade or occupation or into service of anyone under 21. (e) Supply of clothes, linen, bedding, fuel, tools, medical or other aid in sickness, food or other articles in kind. The residue of the income was to be paid in annual pensions to 21 pensioners elected by the trustees and called 'the St Clement Danes Pensioners'.[174]

In 1899 the charity's property produced a total gross annual income of £419 11s. 4d.[175] The amount spent on coal averaged c.£43 during the previous five years.[176] The rent-charges etc. forming the endowments of those charities were paid to the trustees' clerk and the property charge was as follows: £1 from the Saddlers' Co. (Read); 10s. on a house in Holywell St., formerly the Dog Tavern, from the churchwardens of St Giles Cripplegate (Vale and Bissell); 13s. 4d. on no. 219 Strand, from the London & Westminster Bank, Law Court branch (Warner); £3 on 170 Strand, from the receiver of Sergeant Cox's estate (Price); £1 on 279 Strand (Backhouse); £1 on 161a Strand (Margaret Forster); £8 on houses and land in Edmonton, from Messrs. Nicholson and Paterson (earl of Salisbury); and £3 on houses in Milford Lane, from the Arundel Estate office (Mudford). The St Clement Danes Parochial Charities continued in existence until 2007 when they were merged with the Isaac Duckett Charity and St Mary le Strand Charities to form the Strand Parishes Trust.[177] The latter was still in existence in 2018.

173 *Endowed Chars London*, V, 28, 64.
174 *Endowed Chars London*, V, 65–6.
175 *Endowed Chars London*, V, 67–8.
176 *Endowed Chars London*, V, 68.
177 'Strand Parishes Trust', http://www.strandparishestrust.org.uk (accessed 28 Sept. 2013).

St Clement Danes Holborn Estate Charity

The Holborn Estate Charity came into existence on 28 February 1552 when the overseers of the poor decided to buy the Holborn estate from William Breton (or Bretton) for £160. The estate consisted of 12 small cottages, a tenement called the Slaughter House and grazing land situated in High Holborn in the parish of St Andrew Holborn that had formerly been part of the estate of the Carthusian Priory of Charterhouse.[178]

The aim of the charity's founders was to provide alms and accommodation for the poor people of the parish of St Clement Danes. The initial £160 came from the parish rates. The cottages were let and their rents were distributed among the poor of the parish, with others allowed to use the land for feeding and grazing their cattle, as well as the slaughter house, free of charge.[179] The charity was able to enlarge its sphere of activity as more properties were built on the land it owned, increasing its revenue, and as land values in Holborn appreciated.

For a season, in addition to supporting 12 almspeople who were 'decayed' inhabitants of the parish, a portion of the income was applied in liquidation of the poor rates. The charity commissioners deemed the latter use of funds improper and after a court case, a trust deed of 1647 required that almshouses were built on the current site of the Royal Courts of Justice, within a few yards of the east end of St Clement Danes church. The trust deed also ensured that the rents and profits from 1647 to 1679 were appropriated to the benefit of the poor of the parish at large. A suit was brought in 1701 because past collectors for the poor still owed sums on their accounts and money had also been spent on eating and drinking, beadles' salaries, payments to the vestry clerk and other general expenses of the parish.[180] In response, a decree of the Commissioners of Charitable Uses dated 7 February 1701 increased the number of the poor who benefited from 12 to as many who had lived in the parish for more than 12 years, limited only by the profitability of the charity.[181]

The lower churchyard almshouse contained five rooms, with the women receiving 2s. 6d. per week.[182] It remained in use until around 1798 when it was pulled down as part of the widening of the Strand and replacements were built at the back of Clement's Inn Hall.[183] Some houses and ground in Eagle Street were purchased in 1772. A new conveyance to the trustees of the Holborn Estate Charity in 1773 directed that the income was firstly to be distributed in alms to support 12 poor widows in the parish almshouses and the remainder for any public use and benefit of the parish, which the vestry decided to use for repairing the church. Accumulations of income invested in stock amounted to £8,647 in 1814, when part was again used to repair the parish church. A suit was instituted through the Attorney General to force the vestry to use the money for the poor and the Master of the Rolls decreed in 1816 that the whole income should be used to benefit the poor. The trust of 1773, being contrary to the 1701 decree,

---

178 Anson, *The St Clement Danes Holborn Estate Charity*, 6.
179 WCA, 1576/Box 23.
180 TNA, C 93/46/26; C93/49/3.
181 *Endowed Charities*, V, 21–2.
182 Anon., *New Remarks*, 256.
183 WCA, 1576/Box 3 mainly from booklet on 400th centenary of charity; WCA, 1576/Box 12; WCA, St CD Vestry Mins, B1074, 1 May 1798.

was declared void. The income was to be used for maintaining the 12 widows and the almshouses with the remainder to be paid to the overseers of the poor.[184]

In 1819 the income from the charity's property was £3,938 p.a. The almshouses consisted of six tenements under one roof situated at the back of Clement's Inn Hall and abutting on a burial ground belonging to the parish. Each was occupied by two elderly almswomen, appointed by the trustees and churchwardens, who each received 10s. a week and about 10 chaldrons of coals between them. They were attended by two paupers from the workhouse who were paid 4s. a week and £21 was paid to a surgeon and apothecary for daily attendance and medicines. With repairs and water, the total spent on the almswomen was under £400 a year. The remaining income of between £3,400 and £3,500 was paid quarterly to the overseers and carried to the general account of the poor rate. The Charity Commission in 1819 were very doubtful about the justification of using the income to offset the poor rate under the decree of 1816, particularly considering the limitations imposed by the decree, and they submitted the matter to the Attorney General.[185]

During the 18th century, the scope of the charity widened to include the development of local charity schools and was further extended, under the 1844 scheme which followed the long running court case of *Attorney General v Bovill and others*, to both the provision of accommodation for the maintenance of poor people of the parish and education within the parish. It also stipulated that there were to be ten or 12 trustees who were inhabitants and parishioners of St Clement Danes with real property that had a yearly value of at least £30, or were rated for poor relief at a rental of £50 or more. There were also to be up to 24 managers to administer the charity who had to be rated for the relief of the poor of St Clement Danes or within five miles thereof.

Other expenditure included £200 a year in apprenticing poor children aged between 13½ and 14½ whose parents had been poor resident householders for at least five years; £300 a year to King's College Hospital in Carey Street provided the hospital admitted (up to a limit) anybody sent by the charity; £100 a year to the Metropolitan Free Hospital in Carey Street; £100 a year to the Public Dispensary, if it moved to the parish of St Clement Danes; £100 a year to the ladies who formed the society for relieving lying-in-women in the parish of St Clement Danes; and £100 a year to the District Visiting Society for the relief of poor sick persons in the parish. The stipends of the inmates of the almshouse were increased to £30 a year.[186]

By 1844 the boundaries of the Holborn estate ran from 77 to 110 High Holborn on the south side, with the northern boundary being an irregular line along the back of houses in Eagle Street. The 1844 scheme also allowed for 40 new almshouses to be built within six miles of the parish. Once the new almshouses were built, the previous almshouses were to be sold and the proceeds used in the erection and fitting up of the new almshouses.[187] It appears that the old site was subject to a legal tussle between the charity and the parish, possibly regarding the freehold, which resulted in the charity surrendering their interest in the almshouses to the parish.[188] The site was then

184 *Endowed Charities*, V, 21–2.
185 Ibid., 23.
186 WCA, 1576/Box 12.
187 Ibid.
188 WCA, St CD Vestry Mins, B1080, 14 Feb. 1850, 7 Mar. 1850.

Figure 24 *The Holborn Estate almshouses built in Garratt Lane, Tooting, in 1848.*

apparently placed in the hands of the churchwardens as a charitable trust.[189] After failed attempts by the Holborn Estate trustees and the parish to come to some agreement to construct an infant school on the site, the parish decided to operate the building as an 'asylum for decayed housekeepers' with the first group of six elderly women inducted in October 1850.[190]

The Holborn Estate almshouses at the back of Clement's Inn Hall, on the site of Lamb Yard, were moved to Tooting in 1848. Forty new almshouses, designed by architect Robert Hesketh, were built on land at Garratt Lane. The formal opening of the premises was on 12 July 1849.[191] A matron and superintendant were to be chosen from among the almspeople, whose duties included reading prayers to the others each morning.[192] The site at Garratt Lane was sold in August 1965 for £167,500 (a profit of £52,580) and new almshouses were built at St Clement Heights, Upper Sydenham (Kent), for £511,770.[193]

The Public Dispensary moved into the parish in 1850, from Bishop's Court, Lincoln's Inn to leasehold premises in Carey Street. The dispensary provided free consultations and medicine to poor people not in receipt of parish relief, both on-site and if they lived within a defined local area, at people's homes. The Carey Street premises were acquired for the site of the Royal Courts of Justice in 1868 and the dispensary was moved to a new building in Stanhope Street, where it remained for the rest of the century.[194]

Around 1855 the Peacock Inn, 19–20 Houghton Street and 1 and 3 New Inn Passage were acquired.[195] Having built up these significant landholdings, a renewal of the trustees and managers was needed in the 1850s and 1860s. Of the twelve trustees in 1858, five were dead, two were in their seventies and one had been transported for 14

189 Ibid., 21 June 1850.
190 Ibid., 7 Mar. 1850, 21 June 1850, 18 Oct. 1850.
191 WCA, 1576/Boxes 1 & 2; *Endowed Charities*, V, 56–9.
192 WCA, 1576/Box 12.
193 WCA, 1576/Box 20.
194 *Endowed Charities*, V, 74–6.
195 WCA, 1576/Box 86, 105.

years after being found guilty of the unauthorised disposal of securities, along with one of the managers of the charity.[196] The charity's property included the land used for 'The Metropolitan Horse Bazaar', built over in 1867 by the New Royal Amphitheatre, later called the Holborn Stadium, which covered 24–27 Eagle Street, 1–5 Rose Alley, 1–3 Fishers Court and 85 High Holborn. The amphitheatre provided the only stage in London where feats of indoor equestrian daring might be performed.[197]

There were changes to the scheme in 1882 as well as in 1907, when the members who represented the Strand Ward of the City of Westminster were co-opted as managers. The annual income was divided, with £1,500 going to the governors of the educational arm and £300 to King's College Hospital. £100 was provided to the Public Dispensary Fund, provided the trustees of the dispensary furnished such medicines as may be required free of charge for the use of poor people of the parish, sent by managers of the Holborn Estate Charity. The gifts to lying-in-women and the District Visiting Society remained the same. Any surplus income was to be divided into two equal parts, one for the Educational Endowment and the other in purchasing securities. By 1915 the contributions to the King's College Hospital, for lying-in-women and the District Visiting Society had all ceased, although the £100 to the Public Dispensary continued.[198]

Between 1986 and 2012 the Charity disposed of its property. In the year ended 31 December 2012 the charity's income was £787,857 with expenses of £934,063. It had net assets of £13,673,099 of which £890,799 was the almshouses at Sydenham. In 2017, an annual grant of £60,000 was required to be made to the Trustees of St Clement Danes School Charitable Foundation.

Education

There is evidence that at least one school existed in St Clement Danes in the 1660s and 1670s.[199] It was superseded by a charity school that was set up in 1701, with the help and support of the Society for the Promotion of Christian Knowledge, which was independently funded and run by parishioners who entered into a subscription. Funds were also raised through regular charity sermons at the parish church and gifts.[200] The school was managed separately from the vestry by 12 trustees who were all subscribers. It was situated in the new church yard, Portugal Street. It was initially only for 50 boys, but in 1702 was also able to accept 30 girls. By 1714, the school had expanded to 110 pupils, each nominated by a subscriber. Attendees were exclusively Anglican and proof of their baptism had to be provided.[201] The boys were taught reading, writing, arithmetic, mathematics and singing. The girls were taught to read, sew, knit and sing. The children

196 Anson, *The St Clement Danes Holborn Estate Charity*, 20.
197 *The Young Englishman's Journal*, 15 Feb. 1868, II (45), 716.
198 WCA, 1576/Box 24.
199 P. Maplestone, *St Clement Danes School: 300 years of history* (2000), 2; WCA, St CD Vestry Mins, B1060, 6 Sept. 1675.
200 Maplestone, *St Clement Danes School*, 27–8.
201 Ibid., 2–12.

Figure 25 *The schoolroom in Stanhope Street, used from 1821 until its replacement in 1881.*

were clothed in blue.[202] The school trained a few select boys in trigonometry and mathematics so that they could become 'navigation boys' in the Royal Navy.[203]

An infants' school, the 'Horn Book School', opened in 1724 with 30 pupils, called after the single page, most probably made of bone, that the young children learnt the alphabet from by rote.[204] The overseers sent children to the schools from the age of seven, and the entire schooling system was overseen by a committee of trustees.[205] The youngest children were sent to the Horn Book School, then progressed through either of the upper schools and were apprenticed at the age of 14.[206] This triumvirate of schools was, from the 1740s onwards, housed in a single building – the upper floor of the occasional workhouse – which measured 45 ft across its front, with a depth of 21 ft. It was situated 103 ft away from the almshouses on the upper church yard site.[207] After many years of financial difficulty for the schools in the mid 18th century, the building was demolished to make way for a purpose-built workhouse in 1770.[208] The Horn Book School closed at the turn of the 19th century.[209]

By 1815 the parish had established a national school of 350 pupils and an infant school in Hendon, around eight miles away. In 1821 the charity schools and the national school were merged and moved to a new site in Stanhope Street. The merged school

202 Anon., *New Remarks*, 256.
203 Maplestone, *St Clement Danes School*, 8.
204 Ibid., 12.
205 WCA, St CD Vestry Mins, B1062, 6 Jan. 1715; B1063, 16 Jan. 1724.
206 Maplestone, *St Clement Danes School*, 16–7.
207 WCA, St CD Vestry Mins, B1066, 23 Oct. 1740.
208 WCA, St CD Vestry Mins, B1071, 18 Oct. 1770.
209 Maplestone, *St Clement Danes School*, 39.

became an elementary school in 1876, for which new buildings were erected in 1881. The scholars, dressed in their Eton collars and mortar-boards, were at the mercy of local youths from the slums, necessitating occasional police protection, although local children did still manage to storm the school.[210] The Stanhope Street site was demolished in 1904 as part of the Kingsway development and the schools were moved to Drury Lane in 1908 – via a temporary home in Vere Street – where the St Clement Danes Church of England Primary School still stands in 2018.[211] In the 19th century the number of schools in the parish burgeoned along with the population, so that by 1837 there were 34 schools, including one Sunday school, with 1,116 pupils.[212] A comprehensive survey is not possible in the space available; we will concentrate on schools set up by the Holborn Estate Charity in the 19th century.

Under a scheme of 1844, the Holborn Estate Charity began providing £300 a year to the Parochial Charity Schools. It also used part of its accumulated income to set up an educational arm for children of inhabitants of St Clement Danes. This scheme created two schools for poor infants who were two years or older and endowed the schools with £400 a year for their maintenance and support. £1,500 was provided for the purchase of land and building the two infant schools. In addition, a building was to be erected or altered for a commercial (later the grammar) school, provided the Court of Chancery approved the estimates. £600 a year was given for its support, as well as £200 a year for apprenticing poor children. The pupils were between seven and ten years old when they were admitted and had to be children of parishioners and inhabitants of St Clement Danes, or boys who were supported by a guardian or relative who met the other eligibility conditions.[213]

One infants' school opened in Milford Lane in 1853 on the leasehold site of the old rectory house, but there was some delay regarding the others. Under another scheme of 1860, a middle class girls' school was added with £200 a year given for its support.[214] The children at this school were to be between seven and 14 at the date of their admission and were to be children of parents, guardians or relatives of parishioners and inhabitants of St Clement Danes. Eventually five freehold houses at 19–20 Houghton Street and 1–3 New Inn Passage were bought in 1855–8 on two separate sites, with one used for the boys' grammar school, master's residence and offices for the charity, and the other for the middle class girls' school, the second infant school and mistresses' accommodation in Houghton Street. The schools were opened in 1862.[215] A day school for boys was also opened in 1862 with the number of pupils reaching 167 by 1867.[216]

The middle class girls' school opened in 1862 with 57 pupils who were all daughters of tradespeople in the parish.[217] The curriculum was the same as for the grammar school, except that the girls did geometry rather than maths and were also taught domestic

210 R.J.B. Pooley, *The History of St Clement Danes Holborn Estate Grammar School* (n.d.), 53.
211 Maplestone, *St Clement Danes School*, 39–55.
212 *First Report of a Committee of the Statistical Society of London on the State of Education in Westminster, 1837* (1838), 6–7.
213 TNA, C 54/13472, no 13; *Endowed Charities*, V, 42.
214 WCA 1576/Box 4.
215 *Endowed Charities*, V, 42–3.
216 Ibid., 60.
217 WCA 1576/25, 446.

economics, law of health and needlework. Girls between eight and 18 could attend at the same tuition fees as the grammar school. The tuition fees in 1876 were £3 a year for any child of a parishioner admitted before October 1875 and £4 10s. for any admitted after that date, while children from outside the parish were charged £6 and £6 15s. respectively.[218] The girls' school stood three doors west of the boys', at the corner of Houghton Street and New Inn Passage and had four classrooms: two on the ground, one on the first floor and one on the second floor. For both schools, the only playgrounds available were the small yards at the back.[219]

By 1871 the Milford Lane school had become a mixed infant school, with a roll of 54 boys and 46 girls up to eight years old. All the children were taught in one room by one teacher. The premises were described as admirable, with accommodation for 172 pupils, although the instruction was far below the minimum standard of a public elementary school. Some changes were made and the school was later recognised as efficient, with accommodation for 56 infants.[220] By 1871 the Houghton Street school had become mixed and infants, with a roll of 121 boys and 121 girls up to nine years of age, and with attendance of 96 boys and 102 girls in a room suitable for 121 under one teacher. All children attended free of charge, except for three boys from outside the parish. The three Rs, religious instruction and singing were taught. Government inspectors felt they could not recognise it as a public elementary school, as although the schoolroom was well-adapted for teaching infants, it did not have the necessary fittings for a mixed school. The teacher was good at teaching infants, but the exam results showed that instruction for the older children was most unsatisfactory. The school was subsequently submitted as efficient with accommodation for 100 infants.[221]

The passing of the Endowed Schools Act led to a new scheme in 1875 which stated that the St Clement Danes Parochial Charity schools would provide new elementary schools, while the Holborn Estate infants' schools were to be closed, with the buildings used to enlarge the Grammar and girls' schools.[222] The 1875 scheme also created a separate educational endowment trust, with the schools transferring from the charity to the school governors. The 1875 scheme allowed for the school to be expanded to educate 250 boys and 150 girls, and alterations were made to the school around 1877.[223]

As soon as sufficient funds were available (£500 a year was to be put aside), the intention was to enlarge the school premises in Houghton Street so that they could accommodate 250 boys and 150 girls. After defraying management expenses and repair costs, the income was to be split, with three-eighths paid to the girls' school and five-eighths to the grammar school. The headmaster was to receive a salary of £150 a year plus an amount per boy, as well as contributions to a pension fund, provided the governors approved. All boys were to pay tuition fees of between £4 10s. and £8 a year, although the fees of sons – or legal or testamentary wards of inhabitants or ratepayers of St Clement Danes – could be reduced by a third. To be admitted, boys had to be between eight and 17 years old and of good character, with priority given to sons – or legal or

218 *Endowed Charities*, V, 47–8.
219 Ibid., 59.
220 TNA, ED 3/27.
221 Ibid.,
222 *Endowed Charities*, V, 43–6.
223 Ibid., 48.

testamentary wards – of inhabitants or ratepayers. They were taught reading and writing, arithmetic and mathematics, geography, history, English grammar, composition and literature and at least one other language (but not Greek), natural science, drawing and vocal music. If funds permitted, two exhibitions a year could be granted to boys educated at public elementary schools in the parish.[224]

The Milford Lane school closed in 1879 and the premises were sold for £3,550. Pupils transferred to the Houghton Street school.[225] The sale proceeds from the Milford Lane school were used to buy two adjoining houses in New Inn Passage so the girls' school could be enlarged, and the site was further increased with the closure of the infant school.[226] In 1881 the parochial schools were rebuilt, which led to the infant schools in Houghton Street closing and the pupils transferring to the new parochial schools. The land and buildings in Houghton Street and New Inn Passage were vested in the governors of an Educational Endowment Trust.[227] From 1882 the governors of St Clement Danes School were entitled to half the income of the charity that was left after making specified payments, including £1,500 a year to the Educational foundation. The 1875 scheme was subsequently varied in 1904, when responsibility transferred from the charity commissioners to the Board of Education.[228]

In the years preceding 1890, there had been a decline in the numbers attending the schools and the charity commissioners' advice was sought regarding the future administration of the foundation. In 1898 the charity commissioners suggested a scheme to amalgamate the schools with Archbishop Tenison's School and St Martin's Middle Class School for Girls in St Martin-in-the-Fields. The governors were unwilling to proceed because of the anticipated alterations to the area which would take place with the building of Kingsway, which it was thought would greatly improve the neighbourhood and make the existing school more accessible. Between 1898 and 1900 the rolls increased, with the number of boys rising from 37 to 54 and girls from 61 to 83.[229]

In 1898 the school was open to all boys of good character aged between 8 and 17 who resided with their parents, guardians or someone approved by the governors. Tuition fees ranged between £4 10s. and £8 a year, with sons of ratepayers eligible for a one-third reduction. There was a graduated entrance exam, but priority was given to sons or wards of inhabitants or ratepayers of the parish and sons of tenants of Holborn Estate Charity. There was a wide grammar school curriculum including religious education (with a conscience clause). Exhibitions of £100 a year were available up to a maximum of £5 per pupil, with priority given to boys from public elementary schools. There were two annual exhibitions of £20 each for further education for a period of four years. Boys who were under 16 and had attended the grammar school for at least two years were eligible. Prizes and exhibitions totalling £160 a year for the same purpose were available.[230] In 1900 the

224 Ibid., 48
225 WCA, Educational endowment trust governors minutes, 1576/91, 74.
226 Ibid., 135.
227 WCA, 1576/Box 12.
228 1903, per WCA, 1576/Box 24; 1906 per WCA, 1576/Box 33.
229 *Endowed Charities*, V, 60–1.
230 Ibid., 46.

Figure 26 *St Clement Danes Primary school in 2017.*

boys' and girls' schools still stood in Houghton Street, surrounded on the north and west by property of a poor character, much of which was about to be demolished.[231]

In 1900 the girls were taught English, maths, Euclid, French, elemental experimental science, domestic science, drawing and dressmaking. Tuition fees were £4 10*s*. or £3 a year for under eights, with £1 extra per term for piano lessons. In the summer of 1900 there were 83 girls: 14 of them were children of residents, with 60 living within a mile of the school. Nineteen of the girls were under eight, seven were between eight and ten years old, and seven were over 16. The parents were mainly shopkeepers, clerks etc with 10 per cent professional and 10 per cent artisans. Seven girls held scholarships, but no exhibitions to places of higher education had been awarded. Reports on the schools were made annually by independent examiners and these showed that the work and general tone in both schools was steadily improving.[232]

In 1913 the girls' school had 130 pupils, but the Board of Education consented to its temporary closure from 31 July 1916, due to decreased income, until there was no longer a deficit; the girls' school never reopened. In 1915 the Board of Education recognised the boys' school as a public secondary school and it received a direct grant from then until 1926. In 1926 there were 210 boys paying fees, except for some free places and

231 Ibid., 59.
232 TNA, ED 7/84 no. 901.

scholars. In 1928 the boys' school severed its physical ties with the parish and moved to Du Cane Road, Hammersmith, in recognition of the declining population in the Houghton Street area, and to accommodate a greater number of pupils. The school moved to Chorleywood (Herts) in 1975 as a mixed comprehensive. Five governors were still appointed by the trustees of St Clement Danes Holborn Estate Charity.[233] The school was still in Chorleywood in 2018.

233 WCA, 1576/Box 34.

Political Life

ST CLEMENT DANES'S POLITICAL LIFE was coloured by its position near to the border of Westminster and the City and along one of London's major thoroughfares, the Strand. The taverns of the parish were popular gathering points for political meetings. Many residents were heavily involved with Westminster elections. St Clement Danes also witnessed the vibrant street politics of the era and was no stranger to great crowds. It was on the route for many major political processions through London and some of its poorer inhabitants added their number to the London 'mob'.

Between 1660 and 1900, many important changes can be observed in the political life of St Clement Danes. In the 17th and early 18th century the parish hosted many political meetings, clubs and dinners of oligarchic factions of the nobility. The mid 18th century saw the rise of the popular debating club and the proliferation of political associations, meeting in taverns and coffee houses, as well as the zenith of street politics, with numerous crowds and riots. A more populist era of electoral politics was ushered in by the election of Charles James Fox in 1780, who was the first in a long succession of radical MPs.

Toward the close of the 18th century, distinct plebeian political groups emerged, as did local loyalist associations, while the mob declined as a force in London politics.[1] In the 19th century formal political parties grew in importance, while Whig aristocrats were superseded by middle and working-class radicals. Finally, following the Reform Act of 1867, there was a realignment between class and political party. The rise of the middle-class Conservative was typified by local businessman, stationer, bookseller and MP, W.H. Smith.[2] By the end of the 19th century and coinciding with its redevelopment, Westminster had left behind its radical past and become a bastion of Conservatism.[3]

Clubs, Associations and Electoral Politics

The borough of Westminster had a broad franchise of inhabitant householders and building in St Clement Danes helped to boost the growth of the Westminster electorate after the Restoration. The Holles family (the earls of Clare) who built Clare Market used their influence to support country candidates in Westminster. Gilbert Holles' servants featured prominently amongst the supporters of Sir William Waller in 1679.[4] John

1   R. Shoemaker, *The London Mob: Violence and Disorder in Eighteenth-Century England* (2004), ch. 5.
2   Viscount Chilston, 'W.H. Smith (1825–1891), the reluctant statesman', *Parliamentary Affairs*, 13 (1959), 198.
3   Baer, *Radical Westminster*, 12–41.
4   *Hist. Parl. Commons 1660–1690*, 'Westminster'.

Holles, earl of Clare and subsequently the duke of Newcastle, who was made lieutenant of Middlesex between 1689 and 1692 then in 1711, also used his local influence to support candidates such as Sir Henry Dutton Colt who were hostile to the Court.[5]

The parish was home to many important political clubs and societies. In the 17th century, the Kit-Cat Club formed in the pie shop of Christopher Cat, variously placed in Gray's Inn Lane and Shire Lane, who at some point moved to a new establishment near the Fountain tavern, in the western part of St Clement Danes.[6] The Club was a literary and political convivial gathering exclusively for Whigs, and amongst its many founding members were Charles Montagu, 1st earl of Halifax (d. 1715), John Somers, Lord Chancellor between 1697 and 1700 (d. 1716), the architect, John Vanbrugh (d. 1726) and dramatist William Congreve (d. 1729).[7] In the 18th century, the increasing number of members (or perhaps the heat of pie ovens and the appreciation of a good wine cellar) necessitated a move to a larger venue, the Fountain tavern.[8] It had been a meeting place for Whig conspirators before the Glorious Revolution, making it an appropriate venue for the club to organise political opposition to Queen Anne and her favoured Tories.[9]

The Fountain tavern continued to be an important site for clubs and associations and was used for meetings of the Royal Alpha Lodge of Freemasons during the 1720s.[10] Opponents of the first Prime Minister, Sir Robert Walpole, regularly dined at the tavern under the soubriquet of the Fountain Club, and went there to celebrate after ousting him from office in 1742.[11] Another important debating club that met in the parish in the mid 18th century was the Robin Hood Society, held at a house in Essex Street during the reign of George II, and apparently moving to the Robin Hood on Butchers' Row in 1747.[12] The Society was an important early step in the formation of debating club culture and a training ground for the oratorical talents of numerous public figures, the foremost of whom was Edmund Burke.[13] During the 1770s and 1780s the Old Playhouse in Portugal Street was used as a meeting place on election days, as well as the venue for the Select Society debating club.[14]

In 18th-century elections, the commercial character of the electorate of St Clement Danes (and St Mary-le-Strand, which was in the same voting disctrict and is included in all voting figures) translated into strong support for Independent candidates, in contrast to some of the richer Westminster parishes. In 1741 the parishioners voted more than

5   *Hist. Parl. Commons 1690–1715*, 'Westminster'.

6   E. Ward, *The Secret History of Clubs* (1709), 260–1; O. Field, *The Kit-Cat Club: Friends Who Imagined a Nation* (2008), 32.

7   Field, *The Kit-Cat Club*, 33.

8   Ward, *The Secret History of Clubs*, 268.

9   Field, *The Kit-Cat Club*, 113.

10   'Lane's Masonic Records', http://www.hrionline.ac.uk/lane (accessed 1 Oct. 2011).

11   *London Evening Post*, 13–16 Feb. 1742; Phillips, *Mid-Georgian London*, 158.

12   J. Timbs, *Club Life of London with anecdotes of the clubs, coffee houses and taverns of the metropolis during the 17th, 18th and 19th centuries*, I (1866), 196–8; Anon., *The History of the Robin Hood Society* (1764), 117.

13   D.T. Andrew, 'Introduction', *London Debating Societies 1776–1799* (1994), vii–xiii: http://www.british-history.ac.uk/report.aspx?compid=38839, (accessed 28 Feb. 2014); *Connoisseur* XVII, 23 May 1754.

14   *Morning Post and Daily Advertiser*, 11 Sept. 1780; D.T Andrew (ed.), 'London debates: 1779', *London Debating Societies: 1776–1799*, 46–64: https://www.british-history.ac.uk/london-record-soc/vol30/pp46-64 , (accessed 18 Feb. 2014).

three to one in favour of Independent candidates, Edward Vernon and Charles Edwin, although they still narrowly lost to the Court candidates, whose support was much stronger in the western parishes.[15] In the by-election of 1749, Lord Trentham was re-elected after joining the government, but 78 per cent of votes in St Clement Danes were for the Independent candidate, Sir George Vandeput.[16] Strand tradesmen particularly favoured him.[17]

From the 1780s, the parish became a centre for the activities of radical Westminster politicians. The 1784 election was notable for the flamboyant canvassing by Georgiana, Duchess of Devonshire, on behalf of Charles James Fox and the St Clement Danes butchers were identified as a source of support in the campaign.[18] The Duchess engaged publically with voters of all classes and amidst accusations of her swapping kisses for votes, she was depicted fondling a Clare Market butcher in a popular print.[19] However, the divided parish electorate did not work in Fox's favour and support in the parish was not as strong amongst ratepayers as the anecdotes of his wider popularity suggested. Each elector had two votes and while 36 per cent plumped for Fox alone, he only received 28 per cent of the total votes in St Clement Danes, as opposed to 33 per cent in Westminster as a whole. Even the Clare Market butchers who had a vote were not wholly in favour of him.[20]

The Crown and Anchor tavern hosted meetings of the Whig club from 1786, becoming indelibly associated with Charles James Fox, who celebrated his election victories and birthdays there throughout the 1780s and 1790s. He was also one of the most notable attendees of a celebration of the anniversary of the storming of the Bastille in 1791, considered an infamous event in conservative circles and inspiring caricaturist James Gillray to represent the Crown and Anchor as the *Gate of Pandemonium*.[21]

During the 1790s, many more plebeian radical societies were formed, the largest being the London Corresponding Society (LCS). LCS meeting places in the parish included the White Horse public house in White Horse Yard, Robin's coffee house, the Crooked Billet public house in Shire Lane, the Peacock Inn in Houghton Street, the Queen of Bohemia's Palace in Wych Street where the general committee met, and the Crown and Anchor tavern on the Strand, where a general meeting was held.[22] In 1794, the general committee began meeting in a room in Beaufort Buildings in the western part of St Clement Danes. It was above a lecture room, both of which were leased by John

15	N. Rogers, 'Aristocratic clientage, trade and independency: popular politics in pre-radical Westminster', *Past & Present*, 61 (1973), 79.

16	1749 poll book data from Harvey, Green and Corfield, *The Westminster Historical Database*.

17	G. Rudé, *Hanoverian London* (Stroud, 2003), 160.

18	*History of the Westminster Election* (1784), 183, 202, 228, 281, 330, 398.

19	*History of the Westminster Election*, 344; BM Satires 6527, W. Dent, *The Duchess Canvassing for Her Favourite Member* (1784). See also A. Rauser, 'The butcher-kissing Duchess of Devonshire: between caricature and allegory in 1784', *Eighteenth-Century Studies*, 36:1 (2002), 23–46.

20	1784 poll book data from Harvey, Green and Corfield, *The Westminster Historical Database; Hist. Parl. Commons 1754–90*, 'Westminster'.

21	J. Gillray, *Alecto and her Train at the Gate of Pandemonium … or … The Recruiting Sargeant enlisting John Bull into the Revolution Service* (1791), BM.

22	M. Thale (ed.), *Selections from the Papers of the London Corresponding Society* (Cambridge, 1983), 462–3.

Figure 27 *The Wellington Club in 1852, which occupied the building used by the Crown and Anchor Tavern.*

Thelwall.[23] The entire general committee of the LCS was arrested under a general warrant by Bow Street officers and King's Messengers at their meeting room in Wych Street in 1798.[24] The radical Society for Constitutional Information also met at the Crown and Anchor, as did the Friends to the Liberty of the Press.

The Crown and Anchor tavern was used by associations representing both sides in the British debate over the French Revolution. At the same time as radical meetings took place (sometimes literally, with concurrent meetings taking place on different floors), barrister John Reeves held meetings of his ultra-loyalist Association for Preserving Liberty and Property against Republicans and Levellers, which soon became known as the Crown and Anchor Society.[25] The parish was home to many loyalist movements, peaking in the period after the French Revolution. In December 1792 a loyalist association met in the vestry room of St Clement Danes, aiming to suppress seditious writings and unlawful assemblies and expressing their support for 'Constitution, by King, Lords and Commons established'.[26] A General United Society, for supplying British

23   Ibid., 145.
24   Thale (ed.), *The Autobiography of Francis Place*, 176.
25   *Association Papers* (1793).
26   *World (1787)*, 13 Dec. 1792.

troops on the continent met at the Crown and Anchor in 1794, and received a donation of £9 15s. from the parish of St Clement Danes.[27]

Through the first half of the 19th century, Westminster's elections were dominated by radical candidates. As Sir Francis Burdett replaced Fox as the figurehead of radical Westminster in the early 19th century, he also took over the Crown and Anchor as his unofficial headquarters.[28] Rather than travelling to parliament, the processions for the chairing of Burdett when he was elected in several general elections passed along the Strand to finish up at the Crown and Anchor tavern.[29] The St Clement Danes churchwardens protested at the use of a white banner representing the parishes of St Clement Danes and St Mary-le-Strand in Burdett's chairing in 1807, on the grounds they had not given permission, nor did they know of the existence of a parish flag.[30]

In the 1818 election Burdett received a third of the votes in both St Clement Danes and Westminster, while more radical candidates received negligible votes anywhere. Where parish and constituency diverged was in the strong local rejection of the ministerial candidate, Sir Murray Maxwell. He received 31 per cent of the votes in Westminster, but only 26 per cent in St Clement Danes. Almost all of the votes which elsewhere went to Maxwell swung to the Whig candidate Sir Samuel Romilly, who very few voters plumped for, but he received support from supporters of Maxwell and Burdett. The respectable traders of St Clement's remained overwhelmingly independent in their political outlook. Of the 159 men who plumped for Maxwell in the parish, more than a third were professionals or rentiers, as were 40 per cent of those who voted for Maxwell and Romilly in tandem.[31]

The Crown and Anchor was used as a venue for many dinners to celebrate the release of notable radicals from jail, including Burdett, John Cam Hobhouse, William Cobbett, William Holmes and John Ward. However, rifts emerged between patrician and plebeian factions of the Westminster radical movement, among complaints that meetings of radical Westminster electors at the Crown and Anchor were being manipulated and criticism stifled.[32] These splits culminated in the resignation of Liberal MP John Cam Hobhouse and his defeat in the subsequent by-election by a radical candidate in 1833. Hobhouse's removal was orchestrated by the new Westminster Reform Society, whose founding members included the famous radical tailor, Francis Place, and the less well-known Thomas Prout, a perfumer based at 229 Strand.[33] A resident in the parish for 40 years, Prout used St Clement Danes' vestry meetings to advance his radical views and worked to create local branches of Westminster-wide radical organisations.[34] Prout's involvement in both vestry and radical politics appears to have borne fruit; simultaneous petitions were presented to parliament against multiple voting and voting by proxy in

27   *Oracle and Public Advertiser*, 18 Mar. 1794.

28   Diprose, *Some Account*, 53–5.

29   *Morning Post*, 30 June 1807; *Examiner*, 12 July 1818.

30   *Morning Post*, 27 June 1807.

31   1818 poll book data from Harvey, Green and Corfield, *The Westminster Historical Database; Hist. Parl. Commons 1790–1820*, 'Westminster'.

32   B. Weinstein, *Liberalism and Local Government in Early Victorian London* (Woodbridge, 2011), 35.

33   Baer, *Radical Westminster*, 28–9, 211–2.

34   *Morning Post*, 22 Nov. 1830; *Daily News*, 17 Apr. 1849.

Figure 28 *William Henry Smith in 1878, the newsagent who became local MP and was a notable philanthropist in the parish.*

parochial matters by St Clement Danes and the Westminster Reform Society.[35] Prout became chairman of the Westminster Reform Society, 'the dominant political force in Westminster' from 1832.[36]

Political meetings and associations continued to flourish at the Crown and Anchor in the 19th century, addressed by leading radicals such as Major John Cartwright and Henry Hunt.[37] From the 1820s through to the 1840s, many meetings were held at the Crown and Anchor supporting parliamentary reform and revolutionary causes as far-

35   *Standard*, 27 June 1838.
36   Baer, *Radical Westminster*, 29.
37   F.D. Cartwright (ed.), *The Life and Correspondence of Major Cartwright*, II (1826), 161, 170, 290; *The Times*, 14 Sept. 1819.

flung as Spain, Portugal, Greece and Poland.[38] Following the Reform Act of 1832, a new generation of radicals including Daniel O'Connell and Joseph Hume became the leading lights of the tavern.[39] Newer political movements were also accommodated, some with greater female participation such as the Great Temperance Festival held there in 1837.[40] The six points that would comprise the People's Charter were written at the Crown and Anchor in 1838, giving it some claim to be the birthplace of Chartism.[41] The Anti-Corn Law League also met there in 1841, leading to clashes between the two groups.[42] In 1848 the Crown and Anchor gave its premises over to a new social institution, the Whittington Club.[43] More extreme political opinions could be found at the ultra-radical meetings run by Dr Watson at the White Lion in Wych Street.[44]

In the second half of the 19th century, Westminster began a steady transformation from beacon of radicalism to bastion of Toryism, although maintaining its independent spirit. Election of all 24 vestrymen from a 'blue' faction and none from the Liberals in 1856 shows that St Clement Danes was already firmly Conservative.[45] Following the Reform Act of 1867, Conservative candidates found themselves with a greatly increased working class support base. W.H. Smith, whose news agency was based in the Strand next door to the Crown and Anchor tavern, was elected a Conservative MP for Westminster at his second attempt in 1868. He donated heavily to local Conservative party organisations and also contributed to philanthropic endeavours in St Clement Danes. Smith became an MP of the Strand district when it was formed in 1885, which he continued to represent until his death in 1891, leaving behind a Conservative-dominated seat and country.[46] New associations continued to be formed. The Saint Clement Danes Lodge of Freemasons was established in 1871 at the King's Head Hotel, opposite the church.[47]

Street Politics: Crowds, Riots and Festivals

St Clement Danes' position on the major route between the Court and the City made it a witness to numerous grand political celebrations, as well as angry riots. City politicians might be seen travelling west along the Strand on their way to deliver a petition to parliament, while state processions often took the opposite route, the monarch being conveyed from St James's Palace to a service at St Paul's Cathedral or a banquet in the Guildhall. On such occasions, the bells of St Clement's would ring out in competition

38   Cartwright (ed.), *The Life and Correspondence of Major Cartwright*, 385; *Morning Chronicle*, 16 May 1823; *The Report of the 14th Anniversary of the Polish Revolution: Celebrated at the Crown and Anchor Tavern, on 29th November 1844* (1845).
39   *The Times*, 9 Dec. 1832 and 21 July 1835.
40   *The Times*, 27 Dec. 1837.
41   *The People's Charter; With the address to the radical reformers of Great Britain and Ireland and a brief sketch of its origin* (1848), 4.
42   *Northern Star*, 13 Mar. 1841.
43   Parolin, *Radical Spaces*, 175.
44   McCalman, 'Unrespectable radicalism', 80–1.
45   *Daily News*, 23 Feb. 1856.
46   Baer, *Radical Westminster*, 33–41.
47   Diprose, *Some Account*, II, 321.

with the nearby City church of St Dunstan's in the West.[48] Between the two, Temple Bar was used as a site of political pageantry; for Charles II's coronation in 1661 it was decked out as a tropical forest, complete with 'a delightful Boscage, full of several Beasts, both Tame, and Savage'.[49] It was joined by a huge cedar maypole 134 ft high and erected nearby, paid for by parishioners and constructed by sailors, directed by the duke of York.[50] Temple Bar was also the focal point of processions on the anniversary of Elizabeth I's coronation in the 1680s, when effigies of the Pope were carried there and burned before a statue of the late queen, Mary I.[51]

The vibrant street life of the parish became particularly notable thanks to the butchers of Clare Market, known for their participation in public celebrations and contributing their numbers to various crowds. The butchers' infamy stretched back to at least the beginning of the 18th century. One book of 1700 mentioned 'the more Unlucky Mob, drawn out of *Spittle-Fields, Clare-Market, and Sweet St. Giles;* in which parts of the Town, Rude Rogues and Reprobates are as Plenty as Lice in a Campaign'.[52] The butchers instigated numerous mobs and rowdy public spectacles, clashing with constable and bailiffs and occasionally meting out their own rough justice.[53] In one example from 1740, they paraded a grotesque effigy of an Irishman around the streets of London on St Patrick's Day, resulting in clashes with the Irish population that had to be quelled by a troop of musketeers.[54]

The radical tailor Francis Place (1771–1854), who was an apprentice in the area, recounted in his memoirs how gangs of boys built up fires to celebrate 5 November and then fought to steal one another's guy. The butchers' boys of Clare Market were by far the most fearsome.[55] The butchers too were involved in the celebrations, parading through the streets playing their 'famed marrow-bone-and-cleaver music'and building a 'tremendous' fire of their own.[56] The butchers also played their music uninvited outside marriage parties and would not leave until they were given money, in the region of a crown or half-crown.[57] If street children or other musicians interfered with the butchers' serenade, fights sometimes broke out to the consternation of the wedding party and

48   H. Johnson, *Temple Bar and State Pageants: An historical record of state processions to the City of London, and of the quaint ceremonies connected therewith* (1897), 3.

49   J. Ogilby, *The relation of His Majestie's entertainment passing through the city of London, to his coronation* (1661), 33.

50   *The Cities Loyalty Display'd* (1661), 4.

51   *The Solemn mock-procession, or, The Tryal & execution of the pope and his ministers on the 17 of Nov. at Temple-bar* (1680).

52   E. Ward, *A frolick to Horn-fair with a walk from Cuckold's-point thro' Deptford and Greenwich* (1700), 15.

53   *Read's Weekly Jnl or British Gazetteer*, 15 May 1731; *Gazetteer and New Daily Advertiser*, 16 Oct. 1772.

54   *Gentleman's Mag.*, X (1740), 142.

55   Thale (ed.), *The Autobiography of Francis Place*, 66.

56   R. Chambers, *The Book of Days: A Miscellany of Popular Antiquities in Connection with the Calendar, Including Anecdote, Biography, & History, Curiosities of Literature and Oddities of Human Life and Character*, II (1832), 550.

57   R. Termagant, *Have At You All: or, the Drury-Lane Jnl* (1752), 233.

Figure 29 *Sailors attacking the Star in the Strand, the event which sparked the bawdy house riots of 1749.*

occasionally the police, although the spectacle was generally enjoyed by the local community. This tradition was in decline by the middle of the 19th century.[58]

The presence of sailors thanks to the relative proximity of London's docks could also lead to disorder. The bawdy house riots of 1749 began on 30 June, when two sailors visited Peter Wood's brothel on the Strand called the Star. The sailors complained to its keeper that they had been robbed, demanding satisfaction. All they received from the keeper was 'foul Language and Blows'. The sailors returned with a party of their shipmates the following evening and destroyed the brothel, throwing any removable items out into the street to create a bonfire.[59] Neighbours apparently responded not with terror at the riotousness or fear of the conflagration engulfing their own houses, but with 'Glee and Mirth'. Troops were called from Somerset House and the sailors were eventually dispersed late that night. The riots spread and brothels around London were targeted for two more days before the disorder was brought under control.[60]

58 R. Chambers (ed.), *The Book of Days: A Miscellany of Popular Antiquities in Connection with the Calendar, Including Anecdote, Biography, & History, Curiosities of Literature and Oddities of Human Life and Character* (1863), 360.

59 *The Tar's Triumph, or Bawdy-House Battery* (1749), BM Sat. 3036; *The sailor's revenge or the Strand in an uproar* (1749), BM Sat. 3035.

60 Gentleman not concern'd, *The Case of the Unfortunate Bosavern Penlez* (2nd edn, London, 1750), 17–25.

Bosavern Penlez was the son of an Exeter clergyman who had moved to London in 1747 to ply his trade as a journeyman barber and peruke maker. In 1749 he started work as a gentleman's servant and took up lodgings in Wych Street.[61] He was not involved in the bawdy house riots until late in the day, by which time he had drunk a considerable amount.[62] Penlez became embroiled in the crowd assaulting the Star and was found asleep in Bell Yard on the morning of 3 July by two watchmen of the Liberty of the Rolls and St Dunstan's in the West. He had a collection of caps, handkerchiefs and aprons stuffed up his shirt. One of seven men arrested during the riots, Penlez and another man John Wilson were found guilty under the Riot Act and sentenced to death. Following a plea for clemency from the 12 Middlesex jurors, St Clement Danes was the first parish to petition for a pardon. Several other nearby parishes followed suit and Wilson's sentence was respited the night before he was to be hanged. Penlez was hanged on 18 October 1749 and buried at St Clement's Church.[63]

Local people had great sympathy not just with Penlez's plight, but also the sailor's initial attack on the bawdy houses. The parish had long been virulent campaigners against bawdy houses in their locality and were clearly unimpressed with the aggressive intervention by government both during the riots and the subsequent prosecution.[64] Penlez came back to haunt the political establishment. In the Westminster election later in 1749, the government candidate was Lord Trentham, brother-in-law to John Russell, 4th duke of Bedford, the Secretary of State who had allowed Penlez to be hanged. Penlez featured in many of the pamphlets and broadsides printed during the viciously fought election and was even carried in animate effigy through the streets of St Clement Danes, accompanied by a candle-lit procession, during the nights of polling. St Clement Danes was a bastion of support for the opposition candidate George Vandeput, and one election broadside even claimed that 'the Ghost of *Penlez* is to come and give his Vote for Sir *George Vandeput*, attended by the principal Inhabitants of St Clements'.[65] Later that year, Sir Thomas Robinson wrote that 'Penley's Ghost (wch they have carried about in Triumph & surely a high insult on Governmt) has raised more People to vote for St Clems. than there are Houses in the Parish'.[66] Nevertheless, Trentham was elected after much expense and a scrutiny of ballots.[67]

Parishioners continued to be involved in the popular politics of London, such as the demonstrations supporting John Wilkes during the 1760s, when many residents showed their support for his cause by illuminating houses along the Strand. When Wilkes made a court appearance before the King's Bench in Westminster, JPs and constables were stationed in St Clement Danes church for fear of rioting.[68] The butchers of Clare Market were particularly active during the anti-Catholic Gordon riots of 1780, when the house

61   Linebaugh, 'Tyburn', 666.
62   *LL*, 'Ordinary of Newgate's Account', OA174910184910180017, 18 Oct. 1749 (accessed 7 June 2017).
63   *The Gentleman's Mag.* 19 (1749), 474.
64   Linebaugh, 'Tyburn', 676.
65   For voting by parish see Rogers, 'Aristocratic clientage', 79; *T--t--m and V--d-t. A collection of the advertisements and hand-bills, serious, satyrical, and humorous, published on both sides during the election for the City and Liberty of Westminster, begun November 22nd, 1749* (1750), 9.
66   Quoted in Rogers, 'Aristocratic clientage', 100.
67   *Hist. Parl. Commons 1754–90*, 'Westminster' (accessed on 29 July 2017).
68   A.H. Cash, *John Wilkes: The scandalous father of civil liberty* (2006), 212, 214.

of Justice Rainsforth who lived in Stanhope Street, Clare Market was gutted and the contents burned as retribution for committing rioters on previous days.[69] Mobs and public violence dwindled towards the end of the 18th century.[70]

Loyalist activities continued in the parish, throughout the years of war with France, culminating in 1815. The inhabitants of St Clement Danes met in the parish church in 1798 to form an armed association for the defence of the country.[71] Further meetings were held, chaired by a churchwarden and attended by fervent local loyalist John Reeves, where a subscription, method of election and even a uniform, complete with scarlet jacket, white waistcoat and breaches were decided upon.[72] The volunteers were frequently involved in public ceremonies and pageants. The Loyal Association of St Clement Danes were presented with their colours in Gray's Inn Gardens. The colours were consecrated by the minister of St Clement Danes and presented by Miss Edwards, daughter of the captain of the first company of the corps, both of whom lived in Beaufort Buildings. Miss Edwards made a stirringly patriotic speech at the ceremony and considering the extraordinary circumstances, asked that she 'be pardoned for stepping out of the ordinary bounds prescribed by sex'.[73]

The St Clement Danes volunteers assisted in guarding Clerkenwell prison after a disturbance there in 1800 and were stationed in Clare Street to help suppress food price riots later that year.[74] Soon after the riots, a meeting was held in the parish church resolving to avoid the consumption of daily staples such as bread, cheese, meat and milk to assist with shortages.[75] In 1803, the St Clement Danes volunteers participated in a review of all the volunteer corps by the King, in which year they numbered 245 troops ready for action.[76] The St Clement Danes volunteers were absorbed as a distinct company by the Royal Westminster volunteers in 1803, for whom a sermon was preached in the parish church.[77] The men of St Clement Danes continued to volunteer for the army of reserve and other defence forces until the end of the Napoleonic wars.[78]

Temple Bar continued to be of particular symbolic importance as the border between Westminster and the City of London.[79] State events, including proclamations of new sovereigns, declarations of war and of peace treaties (including the end of the American Revolutionary Wars in 1783 and war with France in 1802 to give just two examples), were announced by heralds in a grand procession of Westminster dignitaries.[80] After

---

69 T. Holcroft, *A Plain and Succinct Narrative of the Late Riots and Disturbances in the Cities of London and Westminster, and Borough of Southwark* (1780), 22, 55–6.
70 Shoemaker, *The London Mob*, 151–2.
71 *Oracle and Public Advertiser*, 2 May 1798.
72 *True Briton* (1793), 5 May 1798.
73 *Sun*, 10 June 1799.
74 *Morning Post and Gazetteer*, 16 Aug. 1800; *London Packet or New Lloyd's Evening Post*, 19–22 Sept. 1800.
75 *Courier and Evening Gaz.*, 15 Oct. 1800.
76 *Morning Post*, 28 Oct. 1803; *Newcastle Courant, etc*, 5 Nov. 1803.
77 *The British Critic*, XXIII (1804), 89.
78 WCA, B1310–138S; G. Rudé, *Hanoverian London* (Stroud, 2003), 245.
79 E. Mann, 'In Defence of the City: The gates of London and Temple Bar in the seventeenth century', *Architectural History*, 49 (2006), 83.
80 *London Evening Post*, 14 July 1761; *London Gaz.*, 2 Jan. 1762; *London Evening Post*, 19 Mar. 1763; *London Chronicle*, 4 Oct. 1783; *Morning Chronicle*, 30 Apr. 1802.

passing along the Strand, the cavalcade reached Temple Bar, where it would be stopped and ceremonially allowed entry by a deputation including the City Marshal and the Lord Mayor. If the monarch wanted entrance to the City, the gates were closed and only opened upon the knocking of the royal herald. The Lord Mayor would then present the civic keys and sword to the monarch, who returned them to his safekeeping. Temple Bar was removed in 1877, but this ceremony was still performed at the site for Queen Victoria's Diamond Jubilee in 1897, although without the defunct keys.[81]

81   Johnson, *Temple Bar and State Pageants*, 4.

Parochial Origins and Organisation

THE CHURCH OF ST CLEMENT DANES was probably established by Danish settlers before 1066, and certainly existed by 1173 when Henry II granted it to the Knights Templar. Following their suppression, the advowson passed, via the bishops of Exeter amongst others, into the hands of William Cecil, Lord Burghley, in 1560. It was inherited by his eldest son and later earl of Essex, Thomas Cecil, remaining in the family throughout most of the 17th century.[1] The right of presentation to the Rectory of St Clement Danes remained in the possession of the earls of Exeter during the 18th century. The earls had a tradition of loyalty to the Stuart dynasty and the Church of England. The 5th earl, John Cecil (d. 1700), was a Jacobite sympathiser and became a Nonjuror, as did several of his successors. The family's High Church proclivities heavily influenced the theological and political character of St Clement Danes in the late 17th and 18th century.

Religious Life

From the 17th century onwards, the church had a long tradition of High Church theology. Many of the clergy who served at St Clement Danes were notably extreme High Churchmen, as were visiting preachers and members of the congregation, including numerous Nonjurors.[2] The staunchly royalist rector Dr Richard Dukeson had his parish sequestrated in 1643 but reinstated at the Restoration and then remained there until his death in 1678. He was an enthusiastic supporter of the ecclesiastical changes made by Archbishop Laud.[3]

The High Church theology prevalent in St Clement's was even expressed in the decoration of the church. An altarpiece completed in 1721, which may or may not have contained an image of Charles Edward Stuart, was nevertheless considered improper by the Bishop of London who ordered that it be removed. An anonymous parishioner wrote in support of the Bishop's decision, claiming that 'Crouds of Irreverend Persons, which were ever *pouring* in, came there not to join in *Prayer* with the rest of the Congregation,

---

1   *VCH Middx XIII*, 162–3.
2   R. Sharp, 'The religious and political character of the parish of St. Clement Danes', in J. Clark and H. Erskine-Hill (eds), *Samuel Johnson in Historical Context* (Basingstoke, 2002), 45–8.
3   C.T. Gatty, *Mary Davies and the Manor of Ebury* (1921), 119–23.

Figure 30 *The interior of St Clement Danes church in 1751.*

but to worship their *popish Saint*.[4] Nevertheless, the altarpiece continued to hang in the vestry room until 1752.[5] Curiously, some of John Wesley's earliest sermons were given at St Clement Danes as his father had High Church connections.[6]

Enthusiasm for High Church doctrine and politics extended out into the culture of the parish. During the 18th century, St Clement Danes was home to several publishers with High Church, or even Jacobite sympathies, including Anne Dodd, who was active in the sale and publishing of Tory material between 1719 and 1758, and arrested for circulating a pamphlet in 1737. Tory and High Church dominance of the print market around the parish should not be overstated. There were also several publishers who produced dissenting religious and politically radical material.[7] However, the church itself remained a centre of High Anglicanism. In the early 19th century the St Clement Danes Bible Association met for many years under the presidency of the Revd William Gurney, rector of St Clement Danes, in the Crown and Anchor Tavern, as did the St Clement Danes Ladies' Bible Association.[8] In 1813, St Clement Danes Church hosted a sermon for the benefit of the London society for promoting Christianity amongst the

4   *A Letter From a Parishioner of St Clement Danes, to the Right Reverend Father in God Edmund, Lord Bishop of London, Occasion'd by His Lordship's Causing the Picture, Over the Altar, to be Taken Down* (1725), 6.
5   E.E.C. Nicholson, 'The St. Clement Danes altarpiece and the iconography of post-revolution England', in J. Clark and H. Erskine-Hill (eds), *Samuel Johnson in Historical Context*, 55–6.
6   Rudé, *Hanoverian London*, 107.
7   Sharp, 'The religious and political character of the parish of St. Clement Danes', 48–50.
8   *Morning Post*, 18 Dec. 1822, 28 Jan. 1824.

Jews.[9] Complaint was made in 1842 about the church being flooded with propaganda for an upcoming meeting of the Protestant Association in nearby Essex Hall and advertisements for a sermon by the Revd W. Curling in support of the Association, to be held in St Clement Danes itself.[10]

During the 19th century, the extreme poverty in some sections of the parish and moral panic about the amount of infidelity amongst both rich and poor gave rise to increased interest in missionary work in the parish, with plans made for a second place of worship and a school-church, although both were put on hold due to lack of funds.[11] By 1866, the Clare Market mission chapel had been established in Horse Shoe Court. The building was owned by the Bishop of London's Fund, which also provided a missionary curate. It was supported by donations from local businessmen including W.H. Smith and the Twinings.[12] The building was known as Enon Chapel from 1823, when it was taken over by a group of Dissenters, who also used the vaults beneath as a burial ground. The building was a Temperance Hall for three years from 1844, after which the makeshift graveyard underneath was eventually cleared. It was occupied by various forms of entertainment, including a casino and prizefighting venue, until it was converted back into a chapel.[13]

From 1871, mission services were also held in the St Clement Danes parochial school. The mission ceased in 1894.[14] Another site of Christian moral reform was provided by a Temperance Hall in Portugal Street, where the weekly programme included mothers' meetings, a prayer meeting and a penny savings bank. The hall was set up and run thanks to the 'unwearied zeal and gentle persuasion' of Elizabeth Twining.[15] J.J.H. Septimus Pennington, rector of the parish from 1889, was also dedicated to helping the local poor, as well as commemorating the history of the parish. He commissioned stained glass windows for the church depicting Dr Johnson and other celebrities connected to the parish.[16] However, Charles Booth described Pennington as 'intractable, intolerant and impatient of interference and committee control, capable in his own way, obstinate, and a spender of much money unwisely'.[17] A large parish house was built in Vere Street in 1897. In 1899, the morning congregation numbered around 200 and the evening 400, while the capacity of the church was 1500.[18]

Catholicism

In the 17th century there was a Catholic presence in the parish. Elizabeth Cellier was a midwife, Catholic and resident of St Clement Danes who apparently converted out of loyalty to the Crown during the Civil War and married a Frenchman, Peter Cellier. She

---

9   Ibid., 4 May 1813.
10   *Examiner*, 17 Sept. 1842.
11   *Select Committee into the deficiency of spiritual instruction*, 113–8.
12   Diprose, *Some Account*, 19.
13   Ibid., 83–4.
14   *VCH Middx XIII*, 166.
15   Diprose, *Some Account*, 20.
16   'The Rev. J.J.H. Septimus Pennington', *The Times*, 28 July 1910.
17   LSE, Booth Collection, B244, 193.
18   Ibid.

was falsely accused by a recipient of her charity, Thomas Dangerfield, of conspiring with Lady Powis to help break him out of prison. Cellier was acquitted of high treason in 1680, but found guilty of libel later in the year.[19] It is also likely that several high-profile Catholics congregated around Arundel House in the late 17th century.[20] There were large numbers of recusants across Westminster in the 17th century and 115 presentments were issued in St Clement Danes in one month in 1678. In 1706 there were 148 Catholics listed in the parish, the most of any in London.[21] However, the parish church was a leader in the reaction to Catholicism in the late 17th century with daily public prayers at 8 p.m., 'which never wanted a full and affectionate congregation'. Soon afterwards a monthly lecture was set up which professed 'the true principles of primitive religion', preached by 'eminent divines … from whose lips and pens Popery received such wounds, as all her art will never be able to cure'.[22]

Protestant Nonconformity

Despite the High Church leanings of many Anglicans in the parish, there was still a strong history of nonconformist meetings and preachers in St Clement Danes, with several chapels and meeting houses enjoying a long-standing presence in the area. Westminster offered nonconformists the advantages of a large population with the potential for a bigger congregation and the anonymity of a bustling city. Proximity to the government increased the danger of persecution after the Act of Uniformity in 1662, but also increased the potential of nonconformists to influence political decision-making in their favour.[23]

Presbyterians

In 1672 a licence was granted for a Presbyterian meeting, where William Farrington was preacher, at the Old Playhouse in Vere Street.[24] A Tory campaign against dissenters in 1682–3 led to fines being imposed on the holders and preachers of conventicles in Westminster. Congregationalist minister Richard Stretton was fined for preaching in St Clement Danes in 1682.[25] In 1682, a £320 fine was imposed on Gilbert Holles, earl of Clare, who had allowed the Old Playhouse in Vere Street to be used for meetings.[26] Congregations there ranged between 11 and 25 people.[27] This meeting was also included in a published list of conventicles in London, presumably to aid further harassment. The

19　　E. Cellier, *Malice defeated, or, A brief relation of the accusation and deliverance of Elizabeth Cellier, together with an abstract of her arraignment and tryal, written by herself* (1680); *The tryal and sentence of Elizabeth Cellier for writing, printing and publishing a scandalous libel called, Malice defeated &c…* (1680); *ODNB*, s.v. Cellier, Elizabeth (*fl.* 1668–1688), midwife, (accessed 24 Dec. 2015).

20　　Gatty, *Mary Davies and the Manor of Ebury*, 120.

21　　*VCH Middx XIII*, 196–7.

22　　J. Gillies, *Historical Collections Relating to Remarkable Periods of the Success of the Gospel, and Eminent Instruments Employed in Promoting It*, I (Glasgow, 1754), 440.

23　　*VCH Middx XIII*, 203–4.

24　　*Cal. SP Dom.*, 1671–2, 304.

25　　A.G. Matthews (ed.), *Calamy Revised: Being a revision of Edmund Calamy's account of the ministers and others ejected and silenced, 1660–2* (1934), 467.

26　　*Middx County Rec.*, IV, 177–8.

27　　Ibid., 173.

denomination of the Old Playhouse meeting was listed as 'Pesbyter' and the preacher named as Farindon, presumably a variation on Farrington.[28] Both preacher and meeting were infamous enough to be included in a satirical poem attacking the Whigs:

> Next the *Clare-Market* Priest comes in,
> Who never counted it a Sin
> To lye with Woman, Wife, Maid, Whore,
> And has (they say) bored many a score; ...
> Like *Wanton Priest'* gat *Babe of Grace,*
> But 'twas not ill to ly with her,
> Because a true *Jack Presbyter.*[29]

Nevertheless, dissenters continued to meet in the parish, including a group with unknown affiliation who met in 1691 with the preacher Henry Slade.

A Presbyterian congregation that had been meeting since 1669 in other parts of London built a chapel in New Court, Carey Street which was licensed in 1704 under the preacher Daniel Burgess. Burgess lived locally in Boswell Court until his death in 1713, when he was buried at the church of St Clement Danes.[30] Differences with Burgess led to a large part of the congregation moving to a different meeting, leaving the remainder with significant debts from building the chapel. Greater difficulties were to come. The windows of the building were smashed and the pulpits and pews were torn out and then burnt in Lincoln's Inn Fields during the Sacheverell riots of 1709. The congregation struggled to find funds to fix the damage and were left without a meeting house for some time. Although other Presbyterians eventually helped to pay for the damage, the congregation struggled until the arrival of preacher Thomas Bradbury in 1728. Bradbury brought with him a splinter group from Fetter Lane, insisting that his new congregation become Independents.[31] He remained preacher there until 1759. The chapel was again registered in 1837, as was a Sunday school in 1838. The chapel was closed in 1866, then demolished to make way for the Royal Courts of Justice.[32]

Rather less respectable than Bradbury, John 'Orator' Henley broke with the established church as he was frustrated with his advancement and set up his Oratory, where he charged admission to witness his lively dissenting sermons and apparently had the Clare Market butchers as paid supporters.[33] The most famous site for the Oratory was in Portsmouth Street, Clare Market and then in the disused Lincoln's Inn Fields Theatre. More boisterous than the average church, the Oratory often had a riotous congregation and even a drunken preacher, until his death in 1756.[34]

---

28 *A List of the conventicles or unlawful meetings within the city of London and bills of mortality, with the places where they are to be found as also, the names of divers of the preachers and the several factions they profess* (1683).

29 J. Norris, *A murnival of knaves, or, Whiggism plainly display'd, and (if not grown shameless) burlesqu't out of countenance* (1683), 34.

30 *ODNB*, s.v., Burgess, Daniel (1646–1713), Presbyterian minister (accessed 18 Feb. 2014).

31 *VCH Middx XIII*, 216.

32 Ibid., 207–8; Diprose, *Some Account*, 157–9.

33 *The Gentleman's Mag.*, LVII (1787), 875–6; *Connoisseur*, XVII, 23 May 1754.

34 White, *London in the Eighteenth Century*, 498; *ODNB*, s.v. Henley, John [known as Orator Henley] (1692–1756), dissenting minister and eccentric (accessed 1 June 2017).

Figure 31 *A satire depicting John 'Orator' Henley, preaching at his Clare Market Oratory, with a butcher standing guard.*

Unitarians

There was also a long-standing Unitarian chapel in the parish, which housed 'the first avowedly Unitarian congregation' in the country.[35] It was founded in Essex Street in 1774 by Revd Theophilus Lindsey, who leased a set of former auction rooms. He rebuilt the chapel in 1777 with a minister's house on the ground floor. The first service was attended by many well-known people of the time, including Benjamin Franklin and Joseph Priestley.[36] The congregation flourished in the early 19th century, but had dwindled by the 1880s. The chapel was bought in 1885 by the British and Foreign Unitarian

35   M. Rowe, *The Story of Essex Hall* (1959), ch. 2.
36   T. Belsham, *Memoirs of the Late Theophilus Lindsey* (2nd edn, 1820), 81

Association, remodelled and shared with the Sunday School Association. It was also used as a meeting place for left-wing political groups such as the Fabian Society.[37]

Other Nonconformists

Other nonconformist Protestant meetings in St Clement Danes included the Independents who registered the house of Peter Cuff in Newcastle Court in 1709.[38] Another Independent meeting was held in a house in Wych Street, registered in 1819.[39] Baptists appear to have been a growing presence in the parish in the early 19th century, registering four meeting rooms there between 1818 and 1822.[40] In the 1830s, two Wesleyan meetings were registered in Vere Street and Clement's Lane.[41] Finally, the Rose and Crown in Clare Court, Drury Lane was registered to the Salvation Army in 1894.[42]

37   *VCH Middx XIII*, 220–1.
38   Ibid., 207.
39   Ibid., 207–8.
40   Ibid., 205.
41   Ibid., 214.
42   Ibid., 220.

EPILOGUE

THE ALDWYCH–KINGSWAY DEVELOPMENT COMPLETELY changed the character, land use and population of St Clement Danes. New housing was built across various sites, most of it outside the parish, and was opened to tenants between 1902 and 1906, freeing up valuable commercial space created along the new frontage of Kingsway. Accommodation was provided for 610 people on nearby sites at Duke's Court and 390 people at Russell Court, with a further 680 places at Herbrand Street near Russell Square. All three sites were purchased for £118,400 in 1899 from the duke of Bedford, who bought land to the north-west of Aldwych as part of the deal.[1] Reid's Brewery, at the corner of Gray's Inn and Clerkenwell Roads, was purchased at a cost of £200,000.[2] The site was used to build the Bourne Estate between 1905 and 1909, which housed 1,864 people. 296 people were rehoused in a block in the Millbank Estate. A further 699 people were provided a lodging house at Kemble Street, just west of Kingsway.[3]

This provision was not nearly enough to house all of those people who were displaced, and rental prices were too expensive for the very poor.[4] The Kemble Street lodging house was the only one of these sites within the old parish boundaries, called Bruce House after the chairman of the housing committee. The building incorporated a medical dispensary across four floors which had previously occupied the site, that either had to be rebuilt or compensation paid. Bruce House included such amenities as a reading and a smoking room, but more ominously had a disinfecting chamber in the basement. Each 36ft[2] 'cubicle' cost 7d. for a night, or 6d. if paid for a week, and it was 1d. for a hot bath including soap and a towel. Bruce House was only completed in 1906.[5] The cost per person of rehousing the displaced people in the area was fairly high, but the new housing developments were a financial success for the LCC due to the efficiency of combining the Aldwych–Kingsway development with the Clare Market clearance, the value of the land cleared and the spread of expenditure across the several new developments.[6] All of the developments for which figures are available made a good profit for the Council by 1913–14.[7] Population in the parish continued to decline to 3,152 in 1911 and 1,905 in 1921.[8]

1   M. Stilwell, *Housing the Workers: Early London County Council housing 1889–1911* (2010), 164.
2   *Report from the Joint Select Committee of the House of Lords and the House of Commons on Municipal Trading; together with the proceedings of the committee, minutes of evidence, and appendix* (1900), 286.
3   LCC, *Opening of Kingsway and Aldwych by His Majesty the King*, 11.
4   Durgan, 'Leading the way', 26–7.
5   Durgan, 'Leading the way', 25–6; Stilwell, *Housing the Workers*, 243–9.
6   Stilwell, *Housing the Workers*, 63.
7   Ibid., 169, 172.
8   *Census*, 1911 and 1921.

Figure 32 *An aerial view of Aldwych and Kingsway in 1921.*

Some new buildings were included in the plan for the Aldwych and Kingsway area, including the Strand Board of Guardians in the north of the parish and Carr's Restaurant at the east end of Aldwych.[9] The initial vision of a development fit for the capital of the British Empire was slow to emerge. Many of the sites remained empty for much longer than expected, costing the LCC in lost rates and damaging the economic case for the development. In the Strand, empty space was provided with a fig leaf in the form of possibly the largest ever advertising hoarding in London's history.[10] Sizeable undertakings like Australia House were delayed by the First World War, and it was not completed until 1918. The grand frontages of the new buildings that lined the route, with the specification that they be clad in Portland stone, were not finished until the 1930s with the completion of Bush House and India House.[11]

St Clement Danes was abolished as a civil parish in 1922.[12] Civic pride in the area was not extinguished and in the same year the tradition of beating the bounds of the parish

9   LCC, *Opening of Kingsway and Aldwych*, 15.
10   White, *London in the Twentieth Century*, 362, 8.
11   White, *London in the Twentieth Century*, 8.
12   Youngs, *Guide to the Local Administrative Units of England*, I (1979), 309.

was revived after lapsing for nearly a quarter of a century.[13] The church was hit several times by bombs during the Second World War and while the structure remained sound, the interior was destroyed.[14] The rector of 31 years, William Pennington-Bickford, son in law of the previous incumbent, died soon afterwards, apparently stricken by the damage to his church.[15] His wife, born Louie Pennington, also died later in the year.[16] The church was transferred to the R.A.F. by the diocese of London in 1951 and its restoration, begun in 1953, was funded by the War Damage Commission and the R.A.F. Central Fund, as well as donations from various sources including all R.A.F. units.[17] The restoration was kept as close as possible to Wren's original design and was completed in 1958, when it was reconsecrated in the presence of the Queen. The 735 crests of all the R.A.F units were carved into the floor. The damaged bells were recast and continued to play the tune of the rhyme 'Oranges and lemons, say the bells of St Clemen's', as they had when they were installed at the initiative of Revd Pennington-Bickford in 1919.[18] The statues of Gladstone and Samuel Johnson which stand near the church have since been joined by two of the R.A.F.'s wartime leaders, Air Chief Marshal Hugh Dowding, 1st Lord Dowding, and the controversial head of Bomber Command (1942–46), Sir Arthur Harris.[19]

---

13   *The Times*, 26 May 1922.
14   *The Times*, 11 Feb. 1941.
15   *The Times*, 14 June 1941.
16   *The Times*, 9 Sept. 1941.
17   *The Times*, 26 Oct. 1951 and 23 Sept. 1953.
18   *The Times*, 7 and 20 Oct. 1958.
19   S. Bradley and N. Pevsner, *The Buildings of England, London 6: Westminster* (2003), 291.

ABBREVIATIONS

Abbreviations and short titles used include the following:

Annual Rpt WCC	*1st Annual Report of the Westminster City Council*, (1900)
BL	British Library
BM	British Museum
Bodl.	Bodleian Library
Cal. SP Dom.	Calendar of State Papers, Domestic
Hist. Parl. Commons	http://www.historyofparliamentonline.org/
LCC	London County Council
LL	*London Lives, 1690-1800*. URL: www.londonlives.org, version 1.1, 17 June 2012
ODNB	*Oxford Dictionary of National Biography* (Oxford, 2004; online edn, Oct. 2009) URL: http://www.oxforddnb.com
ONL	W. Thornbury, *Old and New London*, (1878) URL: https://www.british-history.ac.uk/search/series/old-new-london
PA	Parliamentary Archives
Diprose, *Some Account*	J. Diprose, *Some Account of the Parish of Saint Clement Danes (Westminster) Past and Present*, I (1868); II (1876)
StCD Vestry Mins	*St Clement Danes Vestry Minutes*
TNA	The National Archives

VCH Middx II   W. Page (ed.), *A History of the County of Middlesex:*
                                        Volume II: General; Ashford, East Bedfont with Hatton,
                                        Feltham, Hampton with Hampton Wick, Hanworth,
                                        Laleham, Littleton (1911)

VCH Middx XIII   P. Croot (ed.), *A History of the County of Middlesex:*
                                        Volume XIII: The City of Westminster: Landownership
                                        and Religious History (2009)

WCA   Westminster City Archives

INDEX

CPSIA information can be obtained
at www.ICGtesting.com
Printed in the USA
JSHW020942201219
3117JS00003B/5